To Jea

CW00504461

God bless

Jacqueline Fredrickson

JON

A true story of love, courage and faith

Jacky Fredrickson

Jacqueline Fredrickson

JON

A true story of love, courage and faith

MEREO
Cirencester

Mereo Books

1A The Wool Market Dyer Street Cirencester Gloucestershire GL7 2PR
An imprint of Memoirs Publishing www.mereobooks.com

JON: 978-1-86151-493-6

First published in Great Britain in 2015
by Mereo Books, an imprint of Memoirs Publishing

The address for Memoirs Publishing Group Limited can be found at
www.memoirspublishing.com

The Memoirs Publishing Group Ltd Reg. No. 7834348

The Memoirs Publishing Group supports both The Forest Stewardship Council® (FSC®) and
the PEFC® leading international forest-certification organisations. Our books carrying both the
FSC label and the PEFC® and are printed on FSC®-certified paper. FSC® is the only
forest-certification scheme supported by the leading environmental organisations including
Greenpeace. Our paper procurement policy can be found at
www.memoirspublishing.com/environment

Typeset in 12/18pt Bembo
by Wiltshire Associates Publisher Services Ltd. Printed and bound in Great Britain by
Printondemand-Worldwide, Peterborough PE2 6XD

CONTENTS

Acknowledgements
Prologue

PART ONE: THE BEGINNING

PART TWO: DIAGNOSIS

PART THREE: THE WORKING MAN

PART FOUR: DISASTER STRIKES

PART FIVE: THE END

ACKNOWLEDGEMENTS

I would like to thank my wonderful husband Roy for his constant support and encouragement, and my daughters: Rachel for her interest and enthusiasm and Emily for her literary guidance and belief in me. Thank you to my church family for always being there for me when needed.

On Jon's behalf I would also like to thank all the skilled and dedicated medical staff we encountered in the NHS, particularly those working at the Bristol Children's Hospital and the Bristol Haematology and Oncology Centre. In particular I would like to thank Dr Pam Kearns, Dr Kirsten Hopkins and Mr David Porter.

Thank you also to all the charitable organisations that provided support, special experiences and opportunities to meet and make friends with others in similar circumstances, you made such a difference.

For the exceptional care Jon received in his last days at the St. Peter's Hospice, we will be forever grateful.

Thank you.

APRIL 2012

Jon is sitting in his wicker chair in his bedroom. His deep, soulful eyes meet mine across the room and in his rough, scratchy voice he speaks: "It's too late for me, but will you write a book about me when I'm gone?" I smile a sad smile. "I'll do my best Jon! It will be a pleasure."

JULY 15TH 2012

I'm sitting in your wonderful hut Jon, your peace and presence surround me. God bless this writing for you.

x

PROLOGUE

The beginning of the end

It is Wednesday 25th April 2012, and we desperately need some help. Jon is staggering around, his unsteadiness getting worse and worse. Despite the physiotherapist's best and most special mobility aids, we remain worried about him falling. His speech is very slurred and he is so frustrated at not being understood.

Specialist Nurse Lois on the phone agrees to contact St. Peter's Hospice.

The following morning we go shopping to Yate. Jon is getting close to doing all the things on his 'to do' and 'special meals' lists, but he wants new shoes, he wants to go to the bank to find out about making a will, and he wants to cancel his phone contract and get a new one.

We manage the shoes and visit the bank; no joy there over will-making though. We decide to leave the phone, too tired! Not too tired for a mug of hot tea and an iced bun at Parson's Café, however. Jon insists that the wheelchair will be accommodated inside, and of course he's right.

Jon is exhausted now and after a struggle getting upstairs, he falls into bed and sleeps all afternoon.

The Hospice Community Care Nurse rings. She'll come and see us at 2pm tomorrow. 'Great!' I sigh, as I feel a sense of relief wash over me.

On the Friday, Roy and I are increasingly anxious about Jon crossing the landing. We have a rail up the stairs, across the landing and now Roy has bought and attached a sturdy safety gate at the top of the stairs. It doesn't stop us lying awake and jumping out of bed to help each time we hear Jon making his frequent visits to the bathroom in the night.

It is morning and I wake with a start as I hear Jon shouting from his bedroom: "Help!" He has got out of bed and is standing but can't move; with great difficulty I help him to the bathroom. He shuts the door behind him and immediately falls in a heap. He is in a state. He wants to come downstairs, but he's too unsteady. I'm afraid of him falling on top of me, even with two of us helping him.

I manage to persuade him to get back into bed and I bring him some breakfast on a tray.

He is looking forward to a visit from his friends Dawn and Tom. He manages a wash with a bowl of water, dons his favourite Spiderman pyjamas and scrambles back into bed ready for his visitors. He drifts in and out of sleep, despite the loving company who sit beside him and chat.

I ring the Community Nurse and leave a message on

her answering machine. "I am very worried. He has deteriorated since yesterday," I tell her desperately.

She comes early. Assessing the situation in five minutes, she establishes that there is a bed for him in the in-patient unit at the Hospice. She calls an ambulance.

Jon continues to sleep on and off.

I pack a bag of essentials: His breathing pump, medication, PSP, iPod and clean underwear.

The ambulance arrives and Jon makes a token protest, unusually for him. He is not particularly co-operative and takes some long last looks around his bedroom.

"Maybe they will be able to get your symptoms under control and then you'll be able to come home," I try to reassure him. I think we both know that isn't going to happen, but we hang on to hope.

The two paramedics are not prepared to risk getting him downstairs, so they send for assistance. Finally, six paramedics from three ambulances manage to transport him downstairs in a 'striker' – a caterpillar-wheeled chair.

I go with him in the back of the ambulance.

A thoughtful and kind paramedic asks me to tell her about my sleeping son.

PART ONE

THE BEGINNING

Chapter One

AN EVENING
AT THE PUB

March 1985

The swirling mist over the fields was gathering strength and drifting into our path; it was beginning to be difficult to see the road ahead. Roy was muttering. "I'm not keen on this, if we *get* to Burton along these country lanes, in this fog, we may not get back again."

My cautious husband was right; it was looking increasingly as if we were in an aircraft, in the middle of dense cloud. We were heading for an Institute of Road Transport Engineers dinner at Burton on Trent. John Onsworth, a colleague of Roy's, had been extolling the advantages of joining this illustrious group, and we had been invited to their dinner so that Roy could be introduced to some chiefs of the organisation.

A babysitter was cosily watching our television whilst five-year old twins Emily and Rachel were tucked up snugly in their beds. It was a rare opportunity to be out together.

"Let's turn round and go to the Berni Inn instead" I suggested, "we might as well make the most of an evening to ourselves!" Roy readily agreed, and swiftly turned the car around. Heading back the way we had come, we eventually espied the glowing windows that signalled our arrival at the cheerful and lively hostelry.

Like two quite-excited children playing truant, we entered the welcoming Inn and were soon tucking into delicious steaks. It was lovely to have this unexpected time together and we chatted happily about the change of plan and whether Roy's chances of becoming a member of the Road Transport Engineers might have been scuppered. We talked about our lovely girls, and how they were settling in now they were at school.

Our twin girls were gorgeous and we were very happy parents, but the period of their infancy had gone so quickly. Now they were skipping into school eagerly each morning, leaving me with a heavy heart at the school gate. I was harbouring maternal pangs, and longing for that new mother and baby moment all over again. I felt a bit cheated of that new-baby-in-the-cot-beside-you that was the experience of most new mums. Our tiny girls had been

2

seven weeks premature and had needed special care for their first weeks.

"I think it would be wonderful to have just ONE baby, beside me in a cot, and to be able to breast feed from the start," I said. The conversation had inevitably got round to my broodiness. Roy listened and began to see why I felt this way. It was wonderful to have had this chance to talk things through properly, the way you do when sitting opposite at an intimate dinner.

As we left the inn his responses were definitely going in the positive direction. Purposefully we made our way home.

December 11th 1985 – the Flower Club baby

My pregnancy had gone according to plan. It was a joy that the morning sickness which had been such a debilitating feature when I had been expecting the twins had been short-lived. The girls were at school, so during the day I was able to have an afternoon nap and take advantage of the quietness of the house. I was relaxed and happy and the whole family were looking forward to the arrival of our expected baby shortly after Christmas.

The fancy-dress Flower Club party was in full swing, and I was entering into the spirit of things, participating in the games with gusto. A scarf was tied around my eyes and I was spun around. I endeavoured to pin the flower onto its stem; I could hear the happy laughter of the other party-goers, when suddenly there was a whooshing sensation.

"I think my baby may be on its way!" I quietly announced, to everyone's excitement and horror.

My friend Trish, dressed in full green goddess costume, anxiously drove me home. An astonished (and slightly panicking) Roy, who had anticipated having an easy, relaxing evening in front of the television, rushed around gathering things together. He left me to arrange for our neighbour Maureen to step in as an emergency babysitter, whilst he went back hurriedly with the green goddess to collect our car.

Before long we were on our way to Leicester General Hospital. We only just made it. Two rapid hours after my waters had broken, after the shouting and the sweating and the gas and air, the midwife and Roy were both telling me to push, and I was telling them "No, baby's coming without any added assistance!"

The midwife declared, "Well, you have a little boy!"

"Are you sure?" I exclaimed in surprise, "Are you really sure?" I was certain that we would have another girl. It seemed the most likely really. We were both overjoyed. A beautiful, perfect, golden-haired boy. A gift from God.

Then he was weighed and we discovered that he was

only 5lbs. A moment of panic ran through me as I had visions of him being whisked away. "Oh no! Don't let them take him to special care!" I cried. I was fearful that history was about to repeat itself. But no, he was well and healthy and he nestled into my arms. I had my wish, my gorgeous baby by my side, and I was breast feeding happily and hungrily from the start.

When they woke the following morning, the girls were delighted to be told that they had a little baby brother. They were excited to go to school and tell their teacher and classmates, and even more excited to be allowed to come out of school early, after lunch, to visit their new baby brother in the hospital. All the class had made a great big card to welcome him, and Emily and Rachel proudly brought it to show me.

The following day we were discharged and two small girls came to the hospital dressed as proud nurses, ready to help to look after tiny Jon Simon Roy as he arrived home.

Having arrived in time for Christmas meant some quick thinking by Father Christmas, who suddenly had an extra little stocking to fill. Fortunately Baby Jon didn't mind over much about the contents of his stocking, and his big sisters were just relieved that he hadn't been missed out!

As Emily and Rachel were nearly six years old, Jon was born into an already hectic and lively home. It was as well that he was a relaxed and amenable baby, who didn't mind being bundled into the pram or car-seat in order to pursue the busy lifestyles of his big sisters.

Chapter Two

JON BECOMES A
BRISTOLIAN

February 1986

For a while Roy's work responsibilities had changed. He was now the Engineering Manager for the whole of the south, and being based centrally at Halesowen was no longer as convenient. He had quite a choice of locations, but as my parents were living near Cheltenham, it made sense to be closer to them. He decided to relocate his office to Avonmouth near Bristol.

We began to look for a new home. We looked at a variety of places in and around the Bristol area. It was a cold winter and there had been snow falls, but now it had receded to a cold grey slush at the sides of the road. Baby Jon had to accompany us on all our house-hunting expeditions, as he needed regular feeds which only I could

7

supply. We were keen not to prolong these visits and quite soon we settled on a modern house in Chipping Sodbury. It was not quite as big as our house in Leicester, but it was built from a pretty Cotswold stone, and had a lovely location overlooking Sodbury Common.

We now needed to find a suitable school for our girls. We made appointments at all the primary schools in the area and arranged to spend a day looking around, and to show the girls their new home. Rachel was a bit under the weather on the day in question, but was eager to come and view the schools. We visited ALL the schools, went into classrooms, played in playgrounds and had a thoroughly full and interactive day.

Later that evening, getting undressed for bath time, I was alarmed to see that Rachel's back was covered in spots. Big blistery spots! We had inadvertently brought chicken pox to EVERY primary school in Yate and Chipping Sodbury!

Unsurprisingly, three weeks later Emily succumbed to the infection too. I was reassured that baby Jon, still 100% breastfed, would gain immunity to the chicken pox through my antibodies. Maybe if he had had just one exposure that might have been the case, but three weeks after the onset of Emily's chicken pox, little baby Jon was covered in spots.

He was a very poorly baby, hot and bothered, itchy and scratchy. The spots were everywhere, in his mouth and throat and under his nappy. Cuddling and feeding made it worse. The only time he got some respite was in a tepid bath. It was a rather difficult nine weeks of quarantine, and I for one was very glad to see the end of those horrid spots.

The time fast approached when we had to pack up our house in East Goscote and prepare for moving day. We arrived in June. In addition to a furniture removal van, we also had two cars laden with belongings, two little girls, a baby and a cat. Annoyingly, we had to wait to gain access to our new home, the previous occupants being nowhere near ready to hand over the keys. Luckily for us, a kind neighbour across the road saw our arrival and invited us in. We fell on our feet, as a good neighbourly friendship with Pat and Denton had begun. They had two children, Kim and Fergus. Pretty dark-haired Kim was the same age as the girls and they hit it off at once.

September 1986: Baptism, St. John's Church

Jon Simon Roy Fredrickson was baptised in St. John's Church, Chipping Sodbury in September 1986.

We had endeavoured to arrange his baptism at the church in Rearsby, Leicestershire, which attached to the girls' primary school. The vicar called. On seeing our

'For Sale' sign, he encouraged us to wait until we had moved and to seek out a church nearer to our new home. It was good advice, and we were welcomed into St. John's Church in Chipping Sodbury.

Jon's baptism was a special day; it was a meaningful and beautiful service and was attended by many family and friends, including our old neighbours Bill and Maureen, from East Goscote. Maureen had been quite involved throughout my pregnancy with Jon and she had taken it upon herself to knit an elaborate christening gown. Jon was now nine months old and was crawling around, so it was not the most practical of garments. Jon was never one to complain though, and it didn't hamper his movements overmuch. It was a fine and happy day and we enjoyed a party in the garden afterwards. We were glad that Jon had become a member of God's family.

Visits to St. John's Church continued through Jon's childhood. As a baby he came with me to attend school services and concerts for the girls. He often slept, particularly if there was any violin music, which he found particularly soporific. When he was a pupil at the school himself, he had to learn to stay awake!

Loud and tumbling mayhem greeted most mornings as all the preparations for school got underway. Washing, dressing and eating breakfast took place amidst much arguing and panic at lost belongings and forgotten items.

Always the amenable baby, Jon was bundled into the pram or car seat and his needs were largely ignored or postponed until we returned to our now peaceful, calm house.

This was a wonderful time. Jon and I enjoyed everything we did together. Jon loved cooking and regularly stood on a chair to help me make bread. One day we were both shocked when the vibrations of the food mixer, pummelling the dough, caused it all to tumble to the floor with a great crash!

Shopping was another popular pursuit. Jon would chatter away on his 'tin of beans mobile phone' as he was being pushed around in the trolley. "Over and out!" he proclaimed, imitating Daddy on his car phone.

Across the road from our home was the river Frome. On every fine summer's day we packed up our lunch and set off for a picnic on the river bank. The buttercups grew here in great golden profusion and the blond, petite and pretty little Jon created a perfect picture as he ran around and played. He often picked a bunch of the yellow flowers "for mummy".

Near the buttercup meadow, behind a rickety fence, there lived a small family of lively, hungry goats. We stopped to push long grass stalks through the netting. "Maaa! Maaa!" The cheeky Jon would imitate the hungry bleats.

On cooler days we played indoors. Jon enjoyed my undivided attention. If I was having a conversation with a visitor or speaking on the phone, he purposefully climbed upon my lap and firmly put his two little hands across my mouth (smiling at me all the while of course!)

He didn't take no for an answer. "No Jon!" A broad grin and a cheeky face looked at me. Did I mean it? Could he push the boundaries? He was particularly attracted to the bright glass 'coals' on our living room fire. The shiny pieces were irresistible to the inquisitive Jon and no amount of stern warnings had any effect on this toddler with the huge smile and the big blue eyes.

Soon it was time to make our way back up to school to meet the girls. Much as he appreciated the school-time calm, Jon also delighted in meeting his loving big sisters. He loved seeing all the children and knew that the girls would play with him, chat and sing to him and generally be a source of great entertainment when we got home.

Twins with a baby brother were an irresistible magnet to other children. Living in a cul-de-sac it was even more pronounced. Our summer garden was frequently filled with happy, playing children. Jon loved it; his infancy was filled with love and laughter. Roy has fond memories of arriving home from work early on occasions, and a gang of children running towards his car from all directions, with lots of hugs and excited children shouting delightedly.

As time went on, Jon also developed his own special friends, real and imaginary. His best childhood friends were

Michael and Barry. They lived just round the corner and called to play with one another. They played in each other's gardens, climbing and making dens, they built a home-made go-kart that invariably needed mending and took turns riding on Michael's tractor and trailer.

"Uh-oh! It was Pat Rabbit" was Jon's answer to all mishaps. Where Pat Rabbit came from and where he went we'll never know, but this imaginary friend regularly popped into the conversation, particularly if there was a spillage or a toy became broken. He was Jon's foolproof get-out clause!

A more tangible and cuddly friend was 'Spot'. Initially Spot was golden, soft and furry, but he was so loved he eventually became quite flat and not fluffy in the least. He was always needed, whether furry or flat. He snuggled into bed with Jon for many years. He even sneaked away to cub camp, hidden in the bottom of Jon's sleeping bag!

From six months old Jon adored family holidays, usually under canvas, and in all sorts of weather. He loved water and come rain or shine, he couldn't wait to get into the pool, lake, river or sea. He had no fear of being underwater and his favourite trick was his shark impression, as he swam just under the surface with his arm above his head! He loved splashing in the waves and spent hours on his body board as he got older. Children of all nationalities would gather to play together and many

JACQUELINE FREDRICKSON

friends were made on these annual trips to France, Italy and Spain.

Memorably, at one camp site in Northern France he made friends with a freckly-faced boy called James. There was a small lake with boats for campers to use. Jon and his new friend spent hours rowing around the lake, acting as notorious pirates and shouting at one another as though on the high seas. They had such fun and freedom to play.

Chapter Three

GOING TO SCHOOL

Jon had no worries about going to school. He was familiar with the concept, having done the journey twice each day to deliver and collect his sisters. He already knew several of the teachers and many of the children who were to be in his class.

There was security too in knowing that his big sisters were there, albeit in the top junior class. I was not far away either, as I was at that time running the playgroup that operated on the same site.

He was such a friendly child and readily made friends with the whole class. He was frequently invited to play with others after school, and to the many birthday parties.

So it was with some dismay that Jon entered Year One in quite a different way. His new school year was met with tears and anxiety. It was upsetting for me and perplexing.

By a process of elimination we discovered just how important it had been to him to know that we were close by. The girls had now gone on to secondary school and my position as playgroup leader had ended. I was reassured by his lovely teacher that he really was fine after I had gone, but it was a sad parting for the whole of that year. He missed us being there.

Jon was a bright and chirpy boy. He often made amusing observations and frequently made us all laugh. He had good ideas and was intelligent in conversation, so it was disappointing to find that his good ideas didn't always transfer themselves to paper. He found writing physically very difficult and rarely finished any piece of work. His speech wasn't the clearest either; not that we noticed, that was just Jon. He was, however, always 'a pleasure to teach,' 'polite and well mannered', 'popular and friendly'. School reports glossed over his difficulties and left us glowing in our delightful child.

Asthma had also by now become a problem. From three years old he had inhalers and now he needed them at school. He consequently often struggled with elements of PE and was prone to chest infections. On occasion he needed a nebuliser. He was always a 'good patient' and took the medication in a matter of fact way, without complaint.

We discovered that the bouts of asthma were sometimes brought on by proximity to dogs, cats or feathers.

Sometimes it was aggravated by unexpected things, like a whiff of perfume, or a dusty book. He became good at avoiding triggers. It didn't help that his animal-loving sisters had an array of pets. He loved the animals, but had to accept that he needed to keep them at arm's length. This was difficult, especially with guinea pig Nutmeg and rabbit Toggles, who were such friendly little characters.

When Jon was around six years old, Rachel had the loan of a pony called Copper. Jon loved to help to groom him. One day, as a reward for helping, Jon got to have a ride. Copper was very elderly and rather slow, so it was both surprising and alarming when, on feeling the lightweight little boy on his back, Copper decided to gallop off, all around the farmyard. Jon clung on to the front of the saddle as though his life depended on it. He was so relieved to find himself still in one piece when Copper came to a stop. Jon was happy to use his allergies as an excuse never to get too close to horses after that!

Towards the end of Jon's primary school years, Rachel became ill with anorexia. It was a gradual process and it was only as time went by that we began to notice that her weight was steadily falling and she had become pale and listless. Jon was an observer and didn't often comment on things that were happening, but he took it all in. He was worried about his sister. We all were. Unfortunately the less Rachel ate, the more Jon compensated for her. There were always tempting treats around to encourage Rachel to eat. Jon made himself as useful as he could by eating them for her.

He was a caring brother and son, and when things at home were stressful for any reason, Jon made a point of being as helpful and unobtrusive as he could. He was the opposite of demanding. His most used sentence was "I love you!" accompanied of course with a hug.

Secondary school

By mutual agreement we decided that Jon would go to Brimsham Green School. Four years earlier we had moved house from Chipping Sodbury to Yate, and Brimsham Green was conveniently situated a short walk across the road. At the open days, it stood out positively, and Jon was keen to go there. The downside was that his primary school friends were predominantly going to Chipping Sodbury School. This didn't appear to worry Jon. He was friendly and sociable and looked forward to meeting new people.

Secondary schools can be unforgiving places. It was not easy for this slightly out-of-the-ordinary boy to make new friends. Sadly, it doesn't bode well to be an individual; it makes you a target for bullies. We'll never know how much bullying Jon endured. He didn't talk about it. On one occasion when I intervened it seemed to make matters worse. Jon developed strategies for coping. He rarely complained or made a fuss. He did, however, get into some trouble at school, when on one occasion he took matters into his own hands and thumped the bully back, breaking his nose. I think it worked.

Jon really enjoyed cooking (mainly because he so enjoyed eating the results!) He seriously thought he might like to be a chef. The time had come to arrange some work experience and he secured a place at a big hotel. He was nervously looking forward to it and we had tested out the bus route in preparation.

Then disaster struck. On his way home from school, Jon rode his bike down a flight of steps on the footbridge. Was this a regular thing? I don't know, but on this occasion he came off his bike and broke his wrist. The work experience had to be cancelled. He was obviously not intended to be a chef!

February 2001

Bravely, Jon decided he would like to go on the school skiing trip during the February half term. It was completely new to him and a real adventure. He was very excited. A big crowd of other excited young people gathered outside the school, ready for the coach. I waved cheerfully as it set off. Inside I worried nervously about how he would get on.

I think I'd be close to the truth if I said he found it a

big challenge. His balance wasn't good and his energy levels and fitness made the physical demands exhausting, but Jon threw himself into everything and really did his best. At the end of the week he was awarded the prize for the most improved skier!

On the last morning of skiing he fell awkwardly, so he travelled home with a painful knee. As he got off the coach I could see that he was limping. It didn't put him off though and he talked animatedly about going again next year!.

At least he was clean and presentable. A few years earlier, Roy and I had waited for Jon's return from cub camp. We cringed with embarrassment as we saw our unwashed child; he was the grubbiest Cub Scout that you could possibly imagine. Then we realised that actually all the boys were the same. None had seen soap or water for a whole week!

PART TWO
DIAGNOSIS

Chapter Four

NOT JUST
A HEADACHE

December 2001

The next year in Jon's school career was the big exam year. GCSEs loomed large!

The seriousness of this wasn't lost on Jon. He knew the importance of working hard and achieving the best qualifications he could. He got on with his coursework, and did his homework. He thought about the future.

Shortly after his sixteenth birthday, and about a week before Christmas, Jon started to feel unwell. He complained of headaches. One Sunday morning, he was sick. We thought it was probably a virus. The headaches persisted, so we visited the GP. "Pressure of exams, probably" said the doctor. "Working too hard!"

Christmas came. The highlight of the Christmas presents for Jon was a Playstation, and it was a big success.

But Jon still wasn't quite right. He often felt queasy first thing in the morning.

Jon continued to complain of headaches and sickness. At times he lay on his bed clutching his head. We visited the doctor's surgery twice in the following week.

"Too much Playstation!" said one.

"Look at your posture!" said another, "you need to hold your head up properly!"

Well, we had paid Jon's headaches proper attention and seen three different doctors. "There is obviously nothing wrong, Jon," I declared. "Maybe ease up on the school work a bit." Although I didn't really believe he was working THAT hard.

One doctor had issued a prescription for migraine medication, so he took that. He also seemed to have constant hay fever-like symptoms, which seemed to support the virus theory.

Jon muddled through the first half of the spring term. I think he never felt well, but he didn't make a fuss and life was busy. My job was making huge demands on me at that time, so maybe I was preoccupied. Jon was a typical sixteen-year old–who grunted a lot and spent much time in his room.

Despite this, I chide myself; how did I not notice how poorly he was? I think my mum had noticed. She spoke to me at Christmas about it. "He doesn't seem very happy" she noted. "Keep an eye on him, won't you?"

February 2002

Half term came. The headaches were still a problem and Jon started to complain that his eyesight was not quite right. We made an appointment early in the week to see Dr Ward. He was a GP who had known Jon from infancy; he had diagnosed Jon's asthma as a three-year-old. Perhaps he would be more helpful.

On examination, Dr Ward declared, "Probably sinus, also causing the hay fever symptoms." He wrote a prescription for a nasal spray. As a postscript he also suggested that it might be a good idea for Jon to make an optician's appointment. "Maybe the extra school work is straining your eyes?" he suggested.

As soon as we arrived home, we rang the optician. The first available appointment was for Friday 15th February at 4pm. I wrote it on the calendar.

Friday afternoon soon came. Papers littered the dining room table, as I attempted to organise the arrangements for my class to visit the local garden centre the following week.

"I'll walk up to Yate," said Jon, looking round the door at my papery clutter. "Will you meet me at the optician's at four o'clock?"

"Good idea," I agreed. "See you later."

As four o'clock approached I jumped in the car, abandoning my books, and drove to the shopping centre.

Briskly I found my way to the optician's and the waiting Jon. Jon was called, and I settled down to read a magazine. He was some time. 'I guess he's going to need glasses' I thought to myself.

A jittery-looking young optician appears. "Mrs Fredrickson, can you come in?" he asks. I follow him into the poky, dark examination room. He hops from one leg to the other. "I can't find the optic discs!" he exclaims. I don't understand him, but I can see that he is anxious. "I don't know what this means" he admits, "I'm not sure whether to send you to the Eye Hospital." He goes out for a moment.

I'm selfishly thinking of the inconvenience of going to the Eye Hospital, in central Bristol, on a Friday evening. Roy and I had a rare cinema evening planned to see the recently-released *Lord of the Rings*.

Jon and I just look at one another, a bit confused to say the least. The optician returns with a letter in his hand. "I've decided to send you to your GP" he explains, "Take this letter straight there and wait for an answer."

Anxiously we go straight to the doctor's surgery. The receptionist isn't very helpful. I insist that we have to wait until a GP has seen the letter. "I'm not at all sure that that will be possible" she states.

Dr Goodland calls us in at once. He examines Jon and

shines a light into his eyes. "I need to make a phone call" he says hurriedly, and leaves us for a few minutes.

"Frenchay Hospital, Ward 18, they are expecting you" he announces on his return. "Make your way there as soon as you can, take overnight things."

Without discussion we make our way home and pack a rudimentary bag. We are both white. I ring Roy, he's already on his way home, and he answers his mobile phone. "This sounds a bit serious" he says, "I'm nearly home."

We head off to Frenchay Hospital after passing our cinema tickets over to Emily, for her and her boyfriend Paul to use if they wish. We don't say a lot on the way.

They are indeed expecting us on Ward 18. The doctor quickly proceeds to do numerous tests. He looks into Jon's eyes, asks him to walk in a straight line and asks him many basic questions. By 6.30 pm Jon is having a CAT scan and a stunned Roy and I are in the small waiting area, pretending to read through the collection of slightly dog-eared magazines.

Jon is quite amused at having a wheelchair journey to the scanner; he'd walked unaided all the way to Yate only a few short hours before.

Later that evening we are all called into a small room with a doctor, a nurse, and maybe others. We are told that the scan has revealed a growth towards the back of Jon's brain. It is probably a tumour. This is causing a fluid build-up, creating pressure in the brain, hence the headaches and the deteriorating vision.

None of us know how to react to this information. We have absolutely no knowledge of anything like this. We are completely out of our depth. We search unsuccessfully for useful things to say. We do know, however, that this is very serious, and that Jon is going to need surgery to remove this thing very soon. They decide to operate in the morning.

The surgeon, Mr Porter, the gentle giant (as we are to discover) wants to leave the removal of the tumour until the following Monday, when there will be a full complement of back-up and laboratory staff. In the meanwhile it is essential to operate quickly to release the pressure with a drain insertion.

Roy and I leave a pale and slightly bewildered Jon at the hospital. We are unable to stay with him; they offer to attempt to find some accommodation at the hospital for us, but we decide that it's best to go home. We can be back in fifteen minutes if necessary. We try to reassure Jon as best we can, and promise we'll be back early in the morning.

Later that night, Roy and I sit up in bed talking through the dreadful events of the day. It is united and positive talk. A tearful Emily comes in; she hated the film and just wanted to come home. We are in this together. We will all be strong for Jon. I make the decision not to call my widowed mother until the morning. She, at least, might as well have a good night's sleep. We certainly don't and neither does Jon.

We arrive at the hospital early as promised. We meet with the surgeon, and as the whirr of the orderly's vacuum cleaner continues on around us, he explains the details and lists the possible outcomes and dangers of brain surgery. He has a white A4 sheet of paper covered with the risks that he is obliged to tell us about. It includes death. As Jon is under eighteen, one of us has to sign this sheet to give permission for the surgery to go ahead. A brave Roy signs it. I can't, and that sheet of paper will haunt me for some time to come.

Suddenly the girls rush into the ward. Rachel is studying at Worcester University and she has arranged for a friend to drive her home. Then, as a new driver, she does something she has never done before. She backs my car out of the garage, and proceeds to drive herself and Emily to the hospital! They are just in time for hugs all round before Jon is wheeled down to the theatre.

"Remember I love you" Jon says "If I don't survive this."

I retort fiercely "Of course you'll survive! And I love you too."

An anxious few hours followed whilst they drilled into Jon's skull to insert a drain. He was okay, and he did survive.

The indignities of being a hospital patient now kicked in. At sixteen he was so embarrassed by things. Using a urine bottle was the top hate (he never did get used to that!) Now he had a drip stand attached to his skull, so nothing would go over his head.

We had an emergency shopping trip to BWise, at that time the only shop open in Yate on a Sunday that sold pyjamas. They had to be 'old man' style with buttons down the front of the jacket. The girls bought him his first 'Tigger,' bright and bouncy, a good positive statement.

Monday 18th February 2002

First thing in the morning they came for Jon. He was ready to go and a little less nervous than the previous operation, and he had come through that one, so it stood to reason this would be all right. We kissed him farewell and promised to be there when he woke up.

It was a very long day.

We walked the corridors of Frenchay Hospital; we walked through every inch of the grounds. We drank numerous cups of tea in the cafeteria. We didn't talk much. The girls and my now anxious mother waited for phone calls.

Later that evening Jon was transferred to the Barbara Russell Children's Ward for its HDU facilities. There was some initial concern, as it seemed that he was unable to swallow, and I overreacted to the idea of him being fitted with a nasogastric tube. Some small sips of water later and that worry was resolved.

Jon had come through two major brain operations in three days. He was one amazing young man and he had one incredibly skilled surgeon. Thank you, Mr Porter.

The Barbara Russell Ward was bright, colourful and cheery, and we were so pleased that he had been transferred. It was such an improvement on the drab and crowded adult neurology ward, with its badly-fitting metal windows and shabby bed curtains. Sadly, it was only for one night, and then an internal dispute over his care meant that he was returned to the adult Ward 2. It was the first realisation that being sixteen made you neither child nor adult. At least he was allocated a single room, which was a relief to him. Neurology patients can be worryingly unpredictable in their words and actions, and Jon felt safer within his own little space.

We were now looking forward to Jon recovering from his surgery and returning home. Naïvely, we hadn't considered beyond the surgery. Alarm bells rang, however, when a registrar doctor, carrying out a blood test, casually remarked that she needed to contact 'the Oncology Centre'. At this time I knew very little about cancer, but the word 'oncology' caught my attention - wasn't that something to do with cancer?

I rang Roy, who had by now returned to work. "I think you should be here later on when we have the meeting with Mr Porter" I told him. He came at once.

We had assumed that the meeting with Mr Porter was just to give us feedback on the surgery. We could see that it had gone well and Jon was recovering. We hadn't envisaged any other news. How green we were.

So it was that we learned the awful truth that Jon's tumour was a medulloblastoma, an aggressive malignant tumour with a five-year survival rate of 70%. I thought that 70% didn't sound too bad. Not good if you were in the unfortunate 30% who didn't make it, but Jon wouldn't be in that group.

Mr Porter was complimentary about Jon's positive attitude. "He asks all the right questions" he noted. "He is strong and healthy, he'll be all right!"

The word 'malignant' rang in my ears like a heavy tolling and I couldn't escape it. Sixteen-year-old Jon did not realise the significance of this diagnosis. "At least it's not cancer!" he remarked.

Oncology Consultant Dr Kirsten Hopkins came to visit Jon in Frenchay hospital. In a slightly jaunty manner, maybe to disguise the nervousness she may have felt bringing this information to a sixteen-year-old, she began to explain about radiotherapy. She described what would happen, when and how it would be done, and the necessary preparations of head and body moulds to facilitate this. She moved on to the considerable and lengthy description of the probable, the likely and the possible side effects, the immediate and the long-term problems. She talked with rapid fluency for forty-five minutes. We had no questions; we were completely overwhelmed. We just wanted her to stop.

"Do you mind if I have a little time by myself?" whispered an ashen-faced Jon after she had departed. I left him to ponder and absorb the devastating and frightening prospect of all the information with which he had just been bombarded.

Tears ran silently down my cheeks as I sipped my tea in the cafeteria. How were we going to face all the horrors ahead? It seemed an impossible task.

A couple of days later, as we were waiting for a visit from a Dr Steve Lowes, a tall, slim lady knocked on the door. "Hello! I'm Dr Pam Kearns," she explained. "I'm from the Children's Hospital." She had come in place of Steve Lowes. Later we revelled in our good fortune. We loved Pam Kearns and her pleasant, friendly and caring manner. She was brilliant.

She had come to give us all the information about the chemotherapy that was to accompany and follow the radiotherapy. "No! Stop!" pleaded Jon. "Please don't go into detail about the side effects." I explained how hard it had been to take in even a fraction of Kirsten Hopkins' story. "Let's just have the information as we need it," I suggested. She sympathetically agreed.

Jon remained in Frenchay Hospital for another two weeks, gradually becoming more mobile and slowly recovering. I spent my days alongside him, keeping him company and bringing him food. His experience of the food in Frenchay at that time was dreadful. Jon's room was the first one on the right as you entered the ward. As the food was delivered around the ward in a clockwise direction, Jon was always served last. Pretty much all that was left when it got to Jon were the obscure things that no one else had chosen, devilled kidneys or curried eggs. It was lucky that the WRVS shop was not too far along the corridor, selling sandwiches and crisps. Every few days my kind and lovely mum came to visit from Cheltenham. She always brought tasty home-baked things to munch and was great company. Jon and I both loved to see her.

One Sunday, Jon's medical team agreed that he could home for lunch. He was so excited and really looking forward to a home-cooked roast dinner. The day before, Jon had the drain removed from his head, so he could now move freely without having to pull a drip trolley along with him. Shortly after Sunday dinner, we noticed that one side of Jon's face was beginning to swell. The brain fluid was leaking, and collecting under the skin. It was a hurried return to the ward.

33

Before Jon could be discharged he had to endure two really unpleasant procedures. Firstly he had to have his stitches, (actually staples) removed. He had approximately 140 staples holding the edges of his wound in place. A rather nervous-looking student arrived; he had been given the job. He had to learn, but Jon didn't think it was a great decision! Every single staple hurt in that long and painful process, leaving him shaken and sickly. The second was a lumbar puncture. It was required to check the spinal fluid, as the medullablastoma might have travelled down into his spine. Thank goodness the fluid was 'gin clear.'. It was another painful ordeal, and Jon held my hand as he had to lie very still. It was the last time I let him hold my hand whilst he underwent a procedure; he squeezed my hand so hard that the bones overlapped one another. 'Ouch!'

What courage he demonstrated. How brave he was. We were all so full of admiration for him. He endured everything without complaint - he was a star patient.

Chapter Five

PREPARING FOR TREATMENT

At long last Jon could come home. What a sight he was though! His hair had actually needed a cut *before* he went into hospital. Now it was long, unwashed and unkempt, with two shaved areas. Amongst the hair was a thick, yellow sticky unction, dried hard in places, where antiseptic had been used in his two operations. He had asked about his hair when he was told of his diagnosis. "Will my hair fall out?" he asked.

"I'm afraid so!" admitted Mr Porter.

"Well thank goodness it was me that got ill, and not one of my sisters," he remarked, to our surprise. "The girls couldn't cope with losing their lovely long locks." It was an early indication of his thoughtfulness.

I found a mobile hairdresser in the Local Pages

telephone directory and arranged for her to come to our house. She carefully and sensitively addressed the messy, hairy problem and he soon appeared with a clean, shorn head. A great improvement! He decided that he might as well keep his hair very short as it would soon be leaving him anyway. Fortunately, it was quite fashionable and even trendy at that time, thanks to a certain Mr David Beckham. We all thought it suited him very well. I think he quite liked the look too!

Jon had become a sort-of minor celebrity at school. The news of his brain tumour had shaken his peers, as it was beyond their experience. I hope those who had bullied Jon in the past might have had the good grace to feel at least a smidgen of remorse.

Once people heard that he was at home, he had lots of visitors. Cards signed by all his tutor group and teachers arrived. Some visitors came bearing gifts. Jon quite revelled in the novelty of being the centre of attention. However, he was also terribly apologetic, to us, to his nurses, to anyone going to any trouble on his behalf. "Stop apologising, Jon!" we all told him. It was to become a life-long habit. He was so, so, sorry.

The time was fast approaching for treatment to start. Preparations for radiotherapy were arduous and uncomfortable. He had a number of visits to the Oncology

Centre to be fitted for a mask and a full body cushion that was moulded exactly to his shape.

Measurements galore were taken by skilled radiologists, and he even had to have a small tattoo on his back as an aligning tool. He had to lie very still for hours at a time and endure the claustrophobic processes.

I was shut out whilst all this was happening and told to wait outside 'for a few minutes'. I knew how anxious he was, so I sat outside worrying about him.

Over an hour later, I tearfully approached a nurse coming out of the room, "Is something amiss?" I asked. "I was told he would be a few minutes."

"Oh! A few minutes is just a figure of speech," she replied loftily.

Through my tears I asked her, "Have you ANY idea how it feels to have your sixteen-year-old son going through this?"

She thought for a moment. "No," she said "No I hadn't thought about it, I don't know how it feels."

In order to receive the chemotherapy, a line needed to be fitted. It was explained in simple terms by the CLIC (Cancer and Leukaemia in Childhood) nurse at the children's hospital. She had a teddy bear with a line coming out of his chest. His 'wiggly', she called it. Through here all bloods could be taken and medication received. Jon and I were both amused by the term 'wiggly' and chuckled about it after the nurse had gone.

It was a day surgery procedure for the line to be inserted through his chest wall straight into an artery. Now it was the turn of the Children's Hospital nurses to be amused. They didn't recall anyone before having this operation who'd had a hairy chest! For some reason, as the anaesthetic wore off, this wound was excruciatingly painful; Jon reckoned that it was more painful than either of his brain surgeries. It took some hours and several doses of painkiller to get this pain under control, so that we could at last go home.

The next day, radiotherapy started. Jon had to report to the Oncology Centre, at the appointed time, every day for six and a half weeks. I had to quickly get used to city driving (something I would have always avoided previously). Jon was too weak to travel by bus, or to walk from the car park up the hill, so each day we arrived at the Oncology Centre car park half an hour before his appointment. We then sat and waited for a precious space to become available. This was often more stressful than the treatment, and tempers became frayed as people battled for position so they could jump into a space as soon as it became vacant. On most days, twenty to thirty minutes was sufficient, but on a small number of occasions a nervous Jon had to go in alone, leaving me to wait for that elusive spot.

At that time there was always a long wait in the reception area before you were called to go and wait downstairs. It was a good time to tempt Jon's jaded appetite with the deliciously fragrant buns that were generally on sale at the WRVS café. Chelsea buns were especially good as they could be gradually unravelled and tiny curls broken off for small bite-size treats.

All the waiting time was also useful for revision. Those GCSEs were coming and study occupied the mind. What a hard task master I was! But it was good distraction therapy.

It was good to get to know the other patients too. There were the same familiar faces every day and it was good to chat. We were impressed by the amazing upbeat atmosphere that prevailed in the radiotherapy waiting area. Positivity oozed from the larger-than-life characters we encountered. Some were wearing imaginative hats or scarves, but others wore their baldness boldly, almost defiantly. They all had something in common: life was precious.

Jon's first chemotherapy started simultaneously; it was called Vincristine. This was administered at the Children's Hospital, at a ward called Oncology Day Beds. We often had to make our way from there to the Oncology Centre. We discovered that if we went to the BRI (Bristol Royal Infirmary), next door to the Children's Hospital, we could explore the maze of secret passages and lifts that connected it to the Oncology Centre. It was an adventure, *and* it avoided having to climb the steep hill!

The Children's Hospital was light and bright and so very modern. It cheered Jon to hear the familiar voice of 'Wallace' in the lift. "Mind the doors Gromit!" "Doors closing" and "Fifth floor, the yellow floor, mmm... The colour of cheese!" he would say in his unmistakeable Yorkshire accent. It suited Jon's humour, and he often imitated Wallace's stock phrases.

April 2002

On April 18th my mum brought a visitor to see us. His name was Keith, and he was the Minister from her village Free Church. The people of Woodmancote had been so kind. Shocked by my Mum's news of her grandson, they had sent us cards and flowers. Now they had sent their Minister.

Long, lean Keith sprawled comfortably in our conservatory. He was relaxed and had all the time in the world. He drank tea and prayed for us, and with us. He had brought a gift of a book of psalms and a special prayer book for Jon. It felt as if God had entered our house. He was with us and gave me strength and determination. God was on our side.

I had glimpsed God's presence and I wanted to keep it. I decided to visit our local church, St. Mary's in Yate. Perhaps I would find God there? A number of Sundays later I realised that he was in the smiling faces of all the caring people that had started to notice this sad-looking lady sitting alone. They put Jon's name on the prayer list and it had a very positive effect on me to hear his name read aloud during the intercessions. It was good to talk to people after the service over a cup of tea, and the seeds of friendship with some special people were sown.

Jon decided that he would like to come with me. He sat quietly beside me. We don't ever know what is in other people's minds. Was he thinking? Was he praying? He certainly was taking in every word and making it meaningful to him. He was an accomplished listener. His faith journey had begun.

Chapter Six

CHEMOTHERAPY

Jon was to have a cocktail of drugs, three different poisons with specific jobs to do and a whole array of horrible side effects. In order for these to be administered he required hospital admission. The chemo and the subsequent rehydration that was required would take at least two to three days.

The first of these triple chemo hospital stays happened to coincide with the 2002 Football World Cup, which was staged in Korea. A big television screen was set up in the ward to enable the patients to be able to keep up to date with England's progress. The time difference meant that the games were played at rather inconvenient UK times. It felt surreal to be driving into Bristol along deserted roads, at 7.30 in the morning, in order to watch a football match on television in the Children's Hospital.

I got there in time and together with the other children and parents on the ward, we watched the football together. 'Goal!' we shouted excitedly as Michael Owen scored the opener. The dad of the boy in the opposite bed came scurrying through from the kitchen where he had been making his son his breakfast porridge. He had missed it! The only goal!

Jon hated these stays in hospital, which always seemed endless. He experienced various side effects. One of the most worrying was 'rigors'. They started with a small shiver, then gradually, huge, uncontrollable shakes came upon him. He was convinced that he was going to die. "YOU ARE NOT GOING TO DIE!" I shouted. "You are just being dramatic!"

He didn't complain often, but he did feel very rough a lot of the time. He was prone to infections and soreness anywhere and everywhere. This was the start of Jon's preoccupation with personal hygiene. Not something that had ever worried him before! Mouthwash, anti-bacterial hand wash and wipes, frequent tooth brushing, all took on a greater significance. It was as if he could see the germs.

There were two different wards that Jon stayed in. One was a teenage patient ward, where there were other young people being treated for a range of illnesses. The other was specifically for cancer patients. In this ward there was a whole range of ages. Jon at sixteen found it quite hard to have young children and babies around him, as they cried a lot. He was sensitive and it upset him to see such young children having such difficult treatment. He talked about how hard it must be for them, as they wouldn't understand what was happening. He felt grateful that he was old enough to understand. I was grateful too.

Sometimes he had just got comfortable in a particular bed, with his own things around him, when it was necessary for him to be moved to another part of the ward. Jon found this really unsettling. He needed to have some continuity of care to feel safe, and to be able to relax.

The chemotherapy finished and a jubilant Jon thought that it was time to come home, but no, the rehydration that followed could take another couple of days. Jon was so delighted when the time was up and he could come home again. He appreciated his home and loved being back amidst his family.

At this time Jon was also taking his GCSEs. A good outcome of his admission to the Barbara Russell Ward at Frenchay Hospital was that he was referred to the Children's Educational Services. He was eligible for home tutoring.

Gentle tutor Joy with her quiet lilting voice appealed to Jon, and they got on so well. He loved the one-to-one teaching and they built a good relationship. The programme of exams was reduced to the subjects that he could manage. Joy worked with the school in order to finish course work and to prepare him for the examinations. It maybe seemed harsh, but it gave Jon something else to think about. Joy's regular appearances, fitting around hospital appointments, gave the week a sense of routine and normality.

The weeks began to take a shape and we settled into a new 'normal'. On the days that we were at home we had tea and fruit at mid-morning with an accompanying poem. We had a walk, sometimes at the National Trust's Dyrham Park, where we could make our way down to the house on foot, looking out for the elusive deer, then catch the bus back up to the car park after a cup of tea in the cafeteria.

Joy's teaching, visits from the CLIC nurse, short outings and hospital appointments filled our time, and Jon and I began to get to know each other rather well.

Chapter Seven

PROMS
AND HOLIDAYS

The much-anticipated leaver's ball was imminent. Jon hadn't really talked about it, but he knew it was happening. To his delight he was contacted by a group of attractive young ladies from his tutor group. "Hey Jon, we're getting a limo to take us to the leaver's ball, would you like to come with us?" said one of them. Jon smiled broadly. What a question! If their intention was to cheer up this unfortunate young man, it succeeded.

The girls were planning elaborate evening outfits for the occasion. How could he do them justice? He discovered that his dad possessed a no-longer-worn but still-smart dinner suit. He tried it on eagerly, and it fitted him almost perfectly. With a crisp white shirt and a borrowed bow tie, he looked the picture. Now he was excited, and couldn't wait for the evening to arrive.

But the chemotherapy came with many side effects. On the day of the ball, I was pottering in the garden and Jon had been resting upstairs in his bedroom. Suddenly there was an ear-piercing shriek. Dropping my garden trowel, and still wearing my muddy gardening gloves, I raced towards the sound. Jon was lying face down at the bottom of the stairs. It was the first time that the wobbliness that came with the treatment had manifested itself. What a day to choose!

Jon's face was badly grazed as it had skidded across the carpet, but amazingly, other than being shaken up, he was unharmed. As I helped him to his feet his main concern was that he was still able to go to the ball. He wasn't going to miss it! He insisted that he was fine.

He was ready in his suit and looked great, as long as you ignored the red scratches to his face. He had bought pink roses, one for each of his beautiful young lady companions. He carried them confidently. The enormously long white limousine arrived, and Jon climbed on board. Emily and I proudly waved Jon off, with instructions to ring if he wanted to come home at any time during the evening. The limo then left to go to the next address, where there were to be sparkly drinks and a photo opportunity for parents. Emily and I made our way there.

We watched as the ridiculous vehicle arrived, and as the glamorous occupants emerged. What happened next was somehow inevitable. Emily and I could both see that there was a big step out of the car and we could see the danger, but a reluctance to embarrass our boy kept us fixed to the spot. As Jon alighted he sprawled across the pavement, pride sorely dented, and smart trousers ripped! A lesser person would have called it quits, but not Jon, who got up, dusted himself down, pushed away the fuss and proceeded to pose for photos alongside his lovely ladies.

Off they went and we waited anxiously by the phone, anticipating another mishap, but no, he stayed the course.

"I've had a BRILLIANT evening!" he declared triumphantly on his return.

Chemo continued on a three-weekly cycle. It was heavy stuff and Jon was constantly monitored. His blood count, neutrophils and platelets, his hearing and his kidney function were closely watched. He had jaw pains and weak joints; his throat was often sore and sometimes infected with thrush, which made swallowing difficult.

We spent a great deal of time at the Children's Hospital. A pattern emerged. Firstly Jon didn't feel too bad, then he had chemo and his blood count dropped and he became weak and sickly. Gradually it climbed back up and he started to improve until he felt well again, and then it started all over again.

We planned some short breaks to coincide with the

'not-too-bad times'. It was important to have some positive things to look forward to, for all of us. We had planned a special holiday in the South of France for all the family. These plans were aborted early on. Dr Pam Kearns had dismissed the idea as unsuitable shortly after his surgery. We thought that he would have recovered by July. How little we knew!

We had a holiday in Pembrokeshire and chose to stay at a delightful, pretty cottage near Strumble Head. One day into the holiday, Jon started to show a dramatic reaction, sneezing, coughing and wheezing. On close inspection I discovered dog hairs, loads of them, on the settee, rugs and cushions. I vacuumed and cleaned the cottage, but the damage was done, and Jon remained poorly despite antihistamine remedies from the chemist. We contacted the holiday cottage company and asked to be moved, but there was no other cottage available. I wrote in my diary, for future reference, 'DO NOT EVER choose to stay in a property where pets are allowed!' We never have again.

As the next chemo date approached, Jon always became anxious and down in spirits. I employed distraction techniques in order to cope and we played board games, particularly Scrabble, and went for frequent short walks.

Sally and Ali were the CLIC nurses who supported Jon at this time; they visited our home and provided line care. They took the numerous blood samples, and followed up with the results. They talked and they listened, and were absolutely wonderful.

August 2002

Another holiday opportunity presented itself towards the end of August. Learning from the hairy dog cottage, we booked a modern, new, clean house in the New Forest. My lovely Mum was able to come too. We had a beautiful week. Jon managed some short walks through the scenic woodland. Jon's afternoon sleeps could be accommodated and we ate very well, both in the house and out at restaurants.

Most memorable was a wonderful sun-filled day on the Isle of Wight. It was exciting to drive onto the boat for the short ferry journey, and to watch as the island came into view. Much of the day was spent on a glorious sandy beach, where Jon tried his hand at sea fishing from the shoreline. The date coincided with my school's return for the autumn term, I was aware that I was rather fortunate to be spending that day in such a relaxed fashion. A silver lining in the clouds!

Autumn 2002

Chemo continued through the autumn and Jon's mobility

problems increased. He was prescribed some physiotherapy sessions. His physiotherapist, Hannah, was young, blonde, pretty and smiley, and Jon adored her. Physio with Hannah was FUN! She introduced him to the beautiful hydrotherapy pool on the seventh floor of the Children's Hospital. The colourful recessed ceiling lights twinkled down onto the warm waters of the pool. The surrounding walls, adorned with poetry, gave the place a magical quality. It was very special and Jon really enjoyed the experience.

However, even a short spell working in the water exhausted Jon, and getting dressed afterwards was almost beyond him. But it was invaluable therapy and helped to improve Jon's balance and co-ordination. He was always very grateful and appreciative.

Jon continued to have individual tuition at home from Joy. He had been congratulated on his GCSE results by everyone. To have achieved four GCSEs in this year of trauma and intensive treatment was incredible. His school was very accommodating and allowed him to study at home for his remaining GCSEs and in addition, to make a start on a GNVQ ICT course in the sixth form. This meant he could attend school when he was up to it, and to follow his own targets as he was able.

CLIC Nurse Sally came to speak to the sixth form about Jon and his illness. She explained about the treatment and Jon was relieved that people understood his hairless and fragile state.

As time went on, Jon's blood count took increasingly long periods of time to recover and on several occasions his planned chemo had to be postponed. He worked himself up into a state of anxiety, worrying about what would happen next. As the date of the chemo came around he would build himself up mentally to cope with the hospital admission and all that went with that, and then at the eleventh hour it was called off. It was all very stressful!

Chapter Eight

GRANDMA

December 2002

It was a miserable Saturday afternoon and pouring with rain. Tensions were stretched, and Roy was ironing. Unexpectedly, the phone rang.

"Hello, this is Staff Nurse Sue from Cheltenham General Hospital." She had my full attention. "I'm ringing on behalf of your mother. She has been admitted this afternoon."

Apparently she had taken a tumble whilst carrying a chair down the stairs, fallen awkwardly at the bottom and her ankle was broken. She needed surgery. I was told not to worry; my mum was concerned that I had enough to worry about already and that a friend was with her.

We visited her in hospital. She had needed to have an operation, and this, or the medication, had made her sick.

But the ankle was now pinned and plated and just had to heal. "You are lucky not to have done more damage!" I told her.

She came home from hospital and a wonderful army of kind friends helped her get organised. I whizzed across to Woodmancote to do what I could in between Jon's appointments. At her follow-up clinic, Mum was very disappointed to learn that her plaster would not be removed for some weeks, so it was arranged that my brother Andrew would come to collect her and take her back to his home in Hove for a fortnight. After that we planned that she would come to stay with us over the Christmas period. That was the well-thought-out plan.

At 3am on 7th December, the phone beside the bed woke us. We sat up with a start and I answered it. I couldn't believe what my brother was telling me. I screamed in disbelief, stabbing pains shooting through my senses. Our beloved mum and grandma had died.

"She had a broken ankle!" I shouted, "People don't die from a broken ankle!" But she had.

As we prepared for her funeral, amongst the general sorting out of her empty house, the reality of what had happened suddenly hit Jon. His body shook with sobs. It was his first experience of death. It had come too close.

Jon continued to have low blood counts and he needed a platelet transfusion. All went according to plan until we got home. Then, as he was eating his dinner, he was suddenly spectacularly sick. His temperature shot up. The hospital advised us to come straight back in.

A blood infection was diagnosed. No time was lost in hooking him up to an intravenous antibiotic drip, but it was slow to work and he was to spend the next two weeks in the Children's Hospital. It is probably as well that we didn't realise at the time just how serious this was. It could have killed him, or at the very least sent him to intensive care, but he fought it off and made a full recovery.

How I longed to talk to my mum, to pick up the phone and be reassured by her comforting common sense. I cried for the whole of the journey home from the hospital, every day. My grief, pain, and anxiety rolled into one great distress. Mum's support had always been there, how was I ever going to manage without her?

Jon never completed the remaining cycles of chemo. His blood count remained stubbornly low, and routine tests were showing kidney damage. Suddenly treatment was OVER! A little glimmer of light began to shine in a faraway tunnel end.

Chapter Nine

LIFE AFTER TREATMENT

It is strange when life changes suddenly. When you become a patient (or in my case a patient's mum) you plunge straight into an unknown world. You launch yourself out of what you understand as your 'normal life' without time to stop and think. You are catapulted into a world of nurses, doctors, hospital beds, waiting and more waiting. There is a whole new vocabulary, and words you had never heard before start to become familiar. The concepts of things like blood counts start to have meaning.

Unusually for Jon, he found himself the centre of attention. Days began to have shapes, as they revolved around appointments at the Children's Hospital and the Oncology Centre. Home visits from all manner of professional health care workers, the CLIC nurse, the home tutor, the physiotherapist, the occupational therapist and others, created a new 'normal.'

With the end of treatment came euphoria. It was a time for celebrating and sharing the good news. But what then? What happens now? Do you just carry on where you left off as if nothing had happened? Can you pick up the threads of life as it was before?

Jon and I both found this difficult. Neither of us was any longer the person we had been before. The traumas and events of the previous year had changed us and our perception of life.

Jon went back to school, now in the sixth form. School was very accommodating of his needs and allowed him to attend intermittently, as he was able. His tutor Joy still came, as there were the remaining GCSEs to sit. But relationships were different. Jon's experiences set him apart; his view of life was different from the majority of seventeen-year-olds. His energy levels were diminished and he tired very easily.

We had been told that a side effect of radiotherapy to the head was the inability of the body to produce sufficient hormones. The pituitary gland was likely to be severely affected. Tests followed to assess the damage. It appeared that Jon's hormone production was practically nil. A lifelong course of hormone replacements would be necessary.

Jon didn't like the endocrinologist. She was abrupt and she told him very bluntly that his bones had now fused, so he would not grow any more. This meant he was faced with having a maximum adult height of five feet three and a half inches. He found that hard to accept, which made him dislike her even more. The hormone replacement medications were also unwelcome. They consisted of several different tablets taken at different times of day, daily, a self-administered growth hormone injection every day, plus a dose of testosterone, injected at the doctor's surgery every three weeks.

And yet, although he was initially unhappy, once he had accepted the need for these hormones he took them very much in his stride. He organised his medications into daily pill pots and kept a careful diary of his injection dates. The growth hormone had to be delivered and then stored at a cool temperature. The needles had to be discarded into a sharps bin. The collection of this also had to be arranged. Jon took care of that too.

He was most unhappy about the fact that he would not grow any taller. We all tried to make light of the endocrinologist's prediction and tried to give him a little hope, but Jon decided that he would have to be big in other ways. He certainly achieved that!

Chapter Ten

GOD AND GREENBELT

Jon continued to accompany me to church services. His faith journey was just about to really take off with the arrival of new ministers. Dynamic Tim Ashworth had been appointed as Vicar at St. Mary's, and together with his attractive wife Viv, he had started to bring some life and energy into worship. They had teenage daughters (this isn't an insignificant remark!) and they set up a group for young people, 'Sunday @ Seven'. It was perfect for Jon and he went along to the group meetings with great enthusiasm.

At about the same time he became friendly with a Christian girl called Hannah at school. She organised prayer meetings and a Bible reading group at lunchtimes and Jon became drawn into these as well, although he shrank from the evangelical and extrovert form of worship. However, it didn't stop him pursuing an Alpha Course.

His relationship with God, his faith and spirituality, were growing apace, and although he didn't talk about it a lot, it showed in his demeanour and maturity.

He also enjoyed church house groups. Joanne was a young mum and a member of the church community and Jon got on well with her. She hosted a group that met on a Friday morning and Jon started going along, often giving freely of his opinions and contributing ideas and beliefs. I think he spoke more confidently when I wasn't around, so I avoided the temptation of joining him. As we inevitably spent a great deal of time together, it was very good that he had some independent activities that didn't involve me.

Having completed the Alpha Course, the obvious next step was to become confirmed. The day of his confirmation was very special and significant to him. He was so proud and delighted to have a good selection of family members there to support him at the beautiful St. James Church in Westerleigh. It was a beautiful and moving service led by Bishop Mike, the Bishop of Bristol. Jon had developed good relationships within the group attending the preparation classes, so it was decided to carry on meeting together for a follow up Emmaus course. His faith journey continued.

Tim and Viv had been going to the Christian Festival of Greenbelt at Cheltenham Racecourse for many years. They invited Jon to go along with them. He was very excited and couldn't wait to go. Roy and I transported him with his tent, backpack, wellies etc. and deposited the laden Jon with Tim and Viv at the festival entrance.

Roy and I then set off up Cleeve Hill, to visit the special site of my parents' scattered ashes. From up on the hill we were able to look down onto the festival site. The marquees, lights and colourful flags looked so inviting. We were enchanted and vowed to go ourselves the following year.

We have attended every year ever since. At first Jon camped on the festival fields with Tim and Viv, their daughters, and a group of other friends. We, meanwhile, stayed on the adjacent Caravan Club site. Eventually Jon decided to stay with us, sleeping in our awning annexe, and was able to make use of the Caravan Club facilities of hot showers and clean toilets. Quite an improvement on the festival provisions!

Jon adored Greenbelt. He loved the whole festival experience. He enjoyed the lively, interesting and amusing speakers; he loved the stalls selling arrays of bright alternative clothing and hats; the smells of hot dogs and onions, pies and fish and chips. But most of all he loved the music, and it was here that he developed his love of folk music.

He envisaged a time when he would be independent, maybe have his own campervan. He thought about a time when he could be a volunteer and drive people around the festival grounds in the golf buggy taxis.

Some good support systems are in place for young cancer patients. While he was in the midst of treatment, Jon was not up to participating in any of the planned events. But as he started to regain some strength he began to become involved with the TOPS group. This was an offshoot of CLIC, and specifically set up to support teenage oncology patients. Jon benefited from meeting up with others to go bowling or have meals out. They even had a trip to Alton Towers on one occasion. The biggest bonus of this group was the opportunity to make friends with other young people in similar circumstances. They were a mixed bag of young people, but they were fun-loving and all enjoyed some respite from the relentless stress of surgery, treatment and post-treatment problems. Jon made some good friends.

One autumn afternoon during a routine visit from CLIC nurse Sally, I was asked if we felt able to meet up with another teenage oncology patient and her mother. They were feeling isolated and would appreciate some communication with someone going through a similar time. We, of course, were delighted to be asked, and so it was that we got to meet Juliet and her mother, Liz. Juliet was just seventeen when we met. She had just had her birthday and they came to call on us. Juliet was also suffering from a brain tumour and was going through chemotherapy when we met. She and Jon were the same age and got on well. Jon loved having the company of this pretty and pleasant young lady, and I similarly welcomed Liz's friendship. They discovered that they shared the same home tutor, and both had joined the TOPS group, so they went on to spend considerable amounts of time in each other's company.

During the year that followed, Juliet and Liz had some dark and difficult days when Juliet needed more surgery. They were worrying times and Jon and I prayed hard for her safe passage through surgery and recovery. Fortunately our prayers were answered and she came through it all successfully.

In late summer 2003 I was ironing in the kitchen when the phone rang. It was the Sargent social worker from the Children's Hospital. "We've been asked to nominate a young person who we think would benefit from a trip to the Caribbean," she said. "Do you think Jon would like to go?"

I thought it was a joke at first, but no, it was for real. The charity Free Spirit ran amazing, once in a lifetime holidays to the Turks and Caicos Islands. It was to be a three-week trip with an incredible itinerary of special experiences woven into the programme. These included sailing, stargazing, swimming with turtles and rays and flying a helicopter. Jon thought about his response for all of two seconds. It was a fabulous opportunity.

The trip included an introductory weekend to meet and get to know the rest of the group. Jon was delighted to discover that Juliet had been invited as well. It was an excellent trip, and although we actually all missed one another enormously, Jon had a fabulous time and came back with some very special memories, and a very loud shirt!

The reality of the term 'life-threatening illnesses' came a little too close however. One of the boys on the introductory weekend became too ill to go when it came to it, and died shortly afterwards. A heavy cloud hung over us at this news.

Ms Jones, the Head of Year, was very supportive. She had visited Jon at home at the onset of his illness and she talked about 'being creative' when it came to planning Jon's further education. Jon's needs were very individual and she made it possible for these needs to be met.

Jon had embarked on a GNVQ course in IT. This suited him really well, as he could work independently and go into school whenever he was able. For the first time since starting secondary education, Jon loved going to school! After being out of circulation for so long he enjoyed the social interaction. He even ventured into a little romance, giving another dimension to school life! He relished the opportunity to be a boyfriend, even though he did find it a perplexing business, despite having grown up with two sisters!

As part of the IT course Jon needed to participate in some relevant work experience. By using some of his hospital connections he was delighted to arrange a day a week at the CLIC Head Offices. Being able to get himself there on the train added to his sense of independence and he was pleased with himself.

He was given the responsibility of organising the TOPS group. Recruiting new members, arranging outings and the preparation and production of the TOPS newsletter were all in his remit. He threw himself into this challenge with enormous enthusiasm, thoroughly enjoying the office environment and getting on well with the other members of staff. Before long he decided to pursue this path as a career.

PART THREE
THE WORKING MAN

Chapter Eleven

AWARD-WINNING APPRENTICE

After much research, Jon discovered that there was a 'Modern Apprenticeship' scheme in Business Administration, and that really appealed to him. As the end of his extended sixth form approached, he started to explore this avenue. He quickly and easily secured a place for the college part of the apprenticeship, but finding a company to take him on was harder. Jon didn't give in though and followed many leads, eventually coming up trumps with a place at Bristol City Council.

It was perfect! He loved going into Bristol every day and working in the beautiful area around College Green and Park Street. He got on really well with his colleagues and took the traditional apprentice teasing with good grace, even following a request on one occasion to telephone Bristol Zoo, asking to speak to a Mr C. Lyon!

He was lucky that his manager had taken the responsibility for training an apprentice seriously, and she provided him with a terrific range of tasks and experiences, so that he got a complete picture of the diversity of the role of Business Administrator.

Each morning Jon scrubbed up and dressed very smartly, taking great pride in his appearance. He was keen to learn, was polite to everyone and always punctual. His manager Sylvia was so relieved that he was not the typical teenager that she had been dreading!

He also, for the first time ever, excelled at his college work. The learning related totally to the real work that he was doing and that was the key. He got high grades for all his work, which was used by his tutor as an example to others. How Jon grew in confidence! Success breeds success, and that certainly worked for Jon.

Jon's apprenticeship lasted for two years. During that time he initiated ideas that resulted in a significant reduction in paper use throughout the council, and introduced schemes for recycling. He also went on to achieve two levels of NVQs. This success and innovation led to him being nominated and awarded Business Administration Apprentice of the Year in 2005 and 2006. He also won the Chief Executive's Department Young Employee of the Year 2006, and in the same year was presented with an Excellence and Citizenship Award for outstanding achievement at a special ceremony, from the City of Bristol College.

He also had great fun, and introduced his office colleagues to 'Wrong Trousers Day' to raise money for Bristol Children's Hospital. This became an annual event, where the normally conservatively-dressed ladies and gentlemen of his office could be found looking rather silly, wearing shorts or leopard print trousers!

In a perfect world, Jon would have been offered permanent employment as his apprenticeship was completed. In this much less-than-perfect world, the Council was making cuts and not recruiting or replacing staff. Sadly, but inevitably, Jon's time at the Council came to an end.

Three months of unemployment followed. These were tough times, during which Jon's newly-built confidence diminished. He kept a constant watch for available posts and applied for everything that was remotely suitable. Time and again he was invited for interview, but up against eloquent recent graduates, each time he failed to be offered the job.

Eventually, after a long and complicated interview process, he was accepted by the Department for Work and Pensions as an Administrative Officer. After the initial euphoria at becoming a Civil Servant, he discovered, to his dismay, that he was to be based in Bedminster on the other side of Bristol. As the interviews had taken place in central Bristol and Fishponds, he had fairly reasoned that any job he was offered would be based in one or other of those places.

Long winter days followed. A half-hour walk to Yate railway station was followed by a half-hour train journey, and then another thirty-minute walk from Temple Meads brought him to his place of work. We were able to give him a lift at this end on the coldest days, and always on his way home.

Having got used to the journey, he enjoyed the work. He was involved in processing various benefit claims. It was not nearly as interesting or varied as the Council, but he quickly learned what was required and he was comfortable with the repetitive nature of the job. He became a bit of an expert at dealing with funeral payments, and was confident and sensitive when liaising with the bereaved and the different groups of people involved.

On his journey each day he had begun to notice some smart, newly-built riverside apartments. As he walked past them he imagined what it would be like to leave home and become independent.

Jon's opportunity to realise those imaginings came the following summer. Sister Emily had broken up with her long-term boyfriend Paul. She needed to move out of her

Bristol flat and was looking for a housemate. By then Jon's work had been relocated to Fishponds, so a shared house with Emily and another friend, Emma, seemed a very good idea.

The three-bedroomed, bay-fronted house was on the outskirts of Fishponds and was very presentable, having been recently completely refurbished. He was very excited about his move towards independence, and with huge enthusiasm, and quite a lot of help, moved into Oakdene Avenue in September 2007.

Chapter Twelve

INDEPENDENCE

Jon was so proud of his new-found independence. He puffed out his chest and talked about 'my house!' Equipping the house and fitting it out with furniture and curtains was exciting and the three new housemates were buzzing with enthusiasm at the novelty of it all. They went shopping for food together and made plans for regular housemates' dinners, where they would each take a turn in cooking for the others. Jon was in his element and was thoroughly enjoying himself.

It did not take long however, before the plans started falling away and the relationships became strained. It is not easy to share a house with others. Values and priorities are bound to differ and Jon found this hard. Also the practicalities of keeping house, shopping, cooking and laundry came as a shock to his system, although he was good at it. He was determined to eat well. He did not stint on buying good-quality ingredients for meals and he did not hesitate to ring me for instructions on cooking methods and times.

He always took a great pride in his appearance and spent time making sure his shirts and trousers were smartly ironed ready for his working week. He never turned down an offer of help with this though, and liked to come home regularly for a home-cooked meal!

Jon had also taken great pride in growing some facial hair during this year. The golden-red pointy beard was well trimmed and tidy and suited his now stocky frame and shortly-clipped hair style very well. It certainly gave him an individuality and confidence that was satisfying.

Work at the DWP had become a challenge. Despite being within walking distance, which was such a bonus, he started dreading going to work. When he had relocated to Fishponds it had been varied work processing different benefit claims, which he had enjoyed. Now it was turning into a call centre and much of the work involved answering the phone. Thoughtful and sensitive Jon detested the abusive and accusatory calls from irate benefit claimants who were frustrated that their payments had not yet arrived, or were insufficient for their needs. It was so stressful. We talked about developing strategies for dealing with telephone abuse and even threats. He loved it when he could help people and sort out a problem, especially when the caller was appreciative of his efforts, but those calls were very much in the minority.

The atmosphere back at the house was not all rosy either. Jon and Emma had initially got on rather well, but Emma now had a boyfriend. He and Jon did not have any time for one another. Jon felt aggrieved by his attitude towards Emma and hated the fact that he commandeered Emma, the living room, the bathroom or any other space at will. It stopped feeling like his home. Emily also was not there a lot of the time, her boyfriend Bruce was living in Bath, and Emily spent much of her time with him. It wasn't great!

Later, Jon learnt valuable assertiveness skills which would have been useful during this time.

There were fun times too though. We all got on well with Emily's new man, who we all got to know during the memorable Christmas of 2007. New Zealander Bruce, not having been long in this country, and far from home, came with Emily to stay. Rachel also came with her boyfriend, Neill. What a house full! It was a delightful party of a Christmas with lots of laughter, games and walks and good food washed down with ample quantities of wine and cider. We didn't know it at the time, but it was the last Christmas we would ever enjoy quite like that.

We had a family camping holiday the following August

to the Golden Valley near Hay on Wye. It was dreadfully wet and muddy, but still fun and unique in that the whole family were together.

Jon's journey of faith continued to grow during his time in Fishponds. He attended several churches in the vicinity, finally deciding that the worship at St. John's suited him the best. He got to know a number of regular worshippers and was delighted to have a visit from the vicar on one occasion. It was impressive that he made time for building his relationship with God during this busy and difficult year. I think he regarded church as a safe harbour in a choppy ocean.

As September approached, the year in Oakdene Avenue was coming to an end. Emma had left the house already and moved in with her boyfriend, and Emily and Bruce had plans to set off travelling as soon as the tenancy was up.

Jon advertised widely for new housemates in an attempt to stay there, but despite his best efforts, this wasn't to be. The house in Oakdene Avenue had to be cleared and cleaned and everything packed away.

It seemed that Jon was keen to maintain his new-found independence, and liked the idea of a place of his own. We helped him to find a one-bedroomed flat in Fishponds. It had been completely refurbished, and although small, was very smart.

Towards the end of September, on a cool autumn

Saturday, we arranged the moving day. We hired a man with a van to help, and set about with all hands on deck to relocate the furniture from the spacious Oakdene house to the pocket-sized Greenways flat. I stood at the top of the stairs where there was a small left hand bend into the living room. Jon, Roy and 'the van man' attempted to manoeuvre the settee up the stairs. Just before the top it stuck. There was no way it was going to go around the bend. It jammed and couldn't be moved up or down. The beautiful, newly-painted magnolia walls now had a rust-coloured mark which was growing bigger and wider along the path of the settee. The switch for the hall light had now managed to get stuck into the equation also.

As it crunched beneath the settee arms, the lady from the lettings agency appeared at the bottom of the stairs. She had come for Jon to sign the paperwork, acknowledging the excellent state of everything. It would have made a hilarious comedy sketch, if it hadn't been so worrying!

Eventually the idea of getting the settee into the flat was abandoned and the remaining items, boxes and heavy television were crowded into the now full-to-bursting first-floor flat. Jon had a bed, a table and a chair. He had kitchen equipment and some food, so he happily saw us off. We agreed to come back the next day to continue unpacking, and for Roy to fix the broken switch and attempt to cover up the damaged wall paint.

The next day was Sunday and we spent the day helping Jon to unload and sort most of the remaining boxes. As Roy and I left a cheerful and smiling Jon, we remarked to one another how he had never looked happier, or healthier.

PART FOUR

DISASTER STRIKES

Chapter Thirteen

A PHONE CALL
ON THE BUS

At that time Jon was training. He was to be part of the very first team of administrators to put into effect a brand new benefit called ESA. It was due to be introduced in October, and Jon was proud to be part of this team. However, it involved a bus journey into Bristol each day.

On the Monday after he had moved into Greenways, Jon rang me on his way home. He was lost in the maze of residential streets and was wandering. I thought he was ringing me for directions back to his new home.

"I just had a phone call on the bus," he murmured.

"Oh what was that about then?" I replied, sensing the tension in his voice,

"It was from the Children's Hospital," he paused before he finished the story. "They have found something on my scan."

He had had the very last of his regular scans early in August, and had heard nothing, so had not given it any thought. After five years it was just a routine thing. Somebody at the hospital had *just* looked at it, nearly two months later, and discovered something.

"Surely not! They must be mistaken," I say quickly. "You must have moved, it could be a shadow." I am grasping at straws, sensing the panic in Jon's unspoken response.

I drive over to meet him, I find him still walking the streets of Fishponds in a daze. We go back to his flat and talk some more about this devastating turn of events. The plan is for him to have a second scan on Thursday, followed by an appointment with his new Children's Hospital consultant, Rachel. He declines an invitation to return home with me. The happy, smiling young man of yesterday has been replaced by a very different picture.

I rant and rave when I get home. The consultant rings me and I rant and rave some more.

"I cannot cope with this!" I shout, when I come off the phone. Roy says I have to. Defiantly, I continue to alter the curtains for Jon's living room. He *will* be having these!

Thursday comes and Jon has his MRI scan. Jon, Roy and I solemnly go in to see Doctor Rachel. The late effects nurse, Ruth, whom we know well, is with her. She is tearful; she has a box of tissues on the table for us.

Doctor Rachel shows us the scan on the computer. There is no mistake. No amount of fidgeting or shadow could have produced the clear image of tumour re-growth.

We are in despair. It would seem to be the end of the line, but then a glimmer of hope is offered. There is the slightest chance that it might not be a medulloblastoma, but a less aggressive tumour. Doctor Rachel goes on to suggest a plan of action, starting with surgery, and then she goes on to outline a possible treatment that involves high-dose chemotherapy and a bone marrow transplant using Jon's own, harvested, bone-marrow. It sounds horrendous and absolutely, terrifyingly, deadly. We cling to the glimmer of hope.

Jon comes home. He was in his lovely flat for a total of four nights. Now he just wants to be with us.

We go to see Mr David Porter, the neurosurgeon. We have confidence in him and he instils a sense of calm and certainty of success. He does warn us, however, that there are increased risks associated with operating in the same place a second time. There is a greater risk of infection and of things going wrong. He predicts that Jon's mobility may be affected.

"Are we talking a little wobbly, or needing a wheelchair?" I ask him.

"Could be either, or anything in between," he admits.

The dates are arranged and this time Jon is admitted by appointment, to the Neurology Ward 2 at Frenchay Hospital. He seems so well and healthy; it doesn't seem possible that there is a tumour in his brain. He jokes with the nurses confidently and they tease him about putting on his surgical stockings.

Roy and I spend a long day whilst Jon is in surgery. We walk the grounds again and again. We test most of the things on offer in the cafeteria. The sun is warm on this October day, and we sit on a bench soaking it up. For the first time ever I have an overwhelming sense of being wrapped in a blanket of prayer. I know our friends are praying for Jon and for us, I can feel it. I can feel God's presence alongside us.

By teatime Jon is sitting up eating pork casserole. He amazes us. Apart from a huge stapled wound in the back of his head, he looks great. Mr Porter had been to see him and had been pleased with how well he had come through the surgery. He told Jon that the results as yet were inconclusive.

He lied. On our way out to the car park, we bumped into him. "Bad news" he admits, "It is the medulloblastoma again. I didn't want to tell Jon just yet, let him have a night's sleep first." We travelled home in a dark cloud of anger and distress.

At home I picked up a little Mothers' Union prayer

book for people in hospital. It was lying on the table in the conservatory. It fell open at the 'angry prayer'. From my heart I cried it out loud, "Where are you, God?"

Within minutes there was a knock on the front door. Roy brought through a tearful and compassionate Viv. Moments later, Christine, a friend from church, also arrived, with flowers. We hugged and I felt enfolded in care. God's love was right there all the time. "Thank you God, for letting me know!" I whispered when my visitors had gone.

The following day we find a positive and upbeat Jon. He had been considering the options and bravely, he feels certain that he will go down the bone marrow transplant route, if he is able. He had spent some time on the phone, talking to his friend Bryony, who had herself been through this treatment. The alternative was to have some chemotherapy, which would put the cancer on hold for a while.

Then something wonderful happens! Jon's care is transferred to Dr Kirsten Hopkins. At twenty-two Jon is deemed to be an adult and they decide not to treat him at the Children's Hospital any more. Dr Hopkins has other options up her sleeve. She suggests a course of 'stereotactic radiotherapy'. This involves highly-focused beams of radiation targeting the site of the tumour. It is much more specific than the conventional radiotherapy, consequently with less damage to the surrounding brain tissue, and therefore available to Jon. Roy calls her an angel!

Preparation for the treatment includes a trip to Bristol Dental Hospital to take a cast of Jon's teeth. This is used as a base for a metal cage-like contraption that is fitted over Jon's head to provide stability for the radiotherapy. It sounds and looks scary, and Jon is very anxious about the whole idea.

Procedures have streamlined considerably at the Radiotherapy Unit. Predominantly, Jon's appointments are early morning and mostly we are in and out without too much waiting at all. Jon is strong, and well enough to walk down the hill from Trenchard Street car park. After several days of treatment we start to have bets on how long we will be, and whether we will get back to the car park before the next chargeband kicks in. We cheer like excited children when we do it in on time.

Every day for six weeks! We've been here before, and soon settle into a routine. Some days Roy is the chauffeur and I have the day off. A bonus for me!

As the end of treatment is in sight, we start to look forward to the spring and summer holidays. Dr Hopkins has other ideas. She feels that Jon should now have a course of chemotherapy as well. This will continue throughout the summer.

Roy and I feel quite low and depressed at the thought of yet more treatment. Jon, however, just gets on with it without complaint. He is grateful to us for our involvement and always so thankful for the lifts to the Oncology Centre.

Jon's main concern is getting back to work. He has regular visits to meet up with his line manager at Fishponds. He is eager to get back and maybe feels under pressure to do so.

After Jon's re-diagnosis in 2008, Lois, the specialist oncology nurse, suggested that Jon might benefit from some counselling. So it was that Jon was introduced to Hammer Out. This locally-based charity was set up to support people with brain tumours, and part of their support included a number of counselling sessions with an experienced and specially trained counsellor.

Jon was introduced to Kate. This funky and trendily-dressed special lady appealed to Jon at once. Initially she came to our home, and they talked and talked. Sometimes they went for walks and their conversations carried on through the park and back to our living room. I understand that they covered a lot of physical and emotional ground, and Jon really felt the benefit of these sessions. They helped him to voice his worries and concerns. She helped him develop strategies for coping with difficult days. Jon felt that she cared about him and was relaxed in her company. She called herself 'a professional friend, always at the end of a phone'. This was an invaluable service and Jon kept her number ready in his mobile phone.

Chapter Fourteen

BACK TO WORK

In August we had a lovely treat. Jon's sister Emily came home to visit!

At the time of Jon's re-diagnosis she had been in India, and not contactable. When we knew the date of Jon's surgery I sent her a Facebook message. Her last post had been to say that they were about to embark on a Kerala River trip for several days, so would not be online for a while. I worried whether she would see my message before she set off. By amazing good fortune she did, and she rang home at once. She was shocked and horrified, and could not believe what we saying. The Kerala River floated by as she thought of her brother, having surgery back at home.

Now, having settled in New Zealand, and having sorted out her finances and her visa, she was able to pay a flying visit. We had a fabulous, fun-filled fortnight.

Two small proud 'nurses', ready to look after tiny Jon Simon Roy.

Neighbour Maureen had taken it upon herself to knit an elaborate christening gown.

Jon as a toddler, posing with his huge smile and big blue eyes.

Examining a crab in seaside heaven.

Jon had no worries about starting school.

Cowboy birthday party with school friends and big sisters.

New Year's Day 2002, resting a
moment on a walk with Mum
and Grandma.

Ready to be confirmed by the
Bishop of Bristol.

Jon in his tent at the Greenbelt
Festival, Cheltenham.

An exhilarating moment with Bryony
on a CLIC outing to Alton Towers.

Award-winning apprentice with the Lord Mayor of Bristol, Cllr Peter Abraham

Enjoying a family party in November 2007.

We sat on a summit on the Malvern Hills in quiet contemplation
of the rocky road ahead.

A disco night and a log cabin.

Jon and Roy played around together, trying on Isambard's high hat.

A surprise Christmas visit from Bristol Rovers striker Will Hoskins, with Chemotherapy Day Unit staff (photo courtesy of Bristol News and Media)

A truly golden day at Weston-Super-Mare, May 2011.

Trying out a mobility scooter at Westonbirt Arboretum.

A 'Knackered Sailor' at the helm on a Youth Cancer Trust sailing day to the Isle of

Proud brother of the bride at Rachel's wedding on October 8th 2011.

A thoughtful moment on Whitesands Beach on a pilgrimage to
St. Davids, Pembrokeshire.

The whole of London at our feet on a Willow Foundation
trip to London December 2011.

Jon enjoying a pint of cider at the Brimsham.

Jon, the independent travelling man, at Yate Station in January 2012.

Emily exhausted us with her boundless energy and enthusiasm. We planned a day out to Glastonbury, and it was a beautiful summer's day. Despite being in the midst of chemotherapy, Jon seemed well. We climbed Glastonbury Tor, but as we reached the top he became overheated and was suddenly very sick. I mopped him up as best I could with tissues and some bottled water, and we came down again, resting often along the way.

As he cooled down, he soon started feeling better, so we went into a welcoming inn for a sit down and some lunch. It was obviously a day for mishaps, as somehow, Emily managed to spill a half pint of cider into her lap. It looked dreadful! Mopping with tissues really didn't help. The next hour was spent trying on jeans in all the charity shops until she found a pair that fitted. I used to take spare clothes with us when the children were small; I teased them both that I would have to start that up again!

Warm now on the way home, Emily wound down the electric window in the back of the car. Not being accustomed to being opened, this window decided to jam and wouldn't go back up again. We drove home with excellent ventilation! It was a memorable day, filled with laughter.

Rachel and Neill also came to visit while Emily was with us. They were on their return from a riding holiday in the Radnor Hills, and called in for an extended lunch party. It was a beautiful summer's day and we sat in the garden. It was so very special to have all the family back together again.

September 2009

Jon's chemo had finished at the end of August, and he was itching to get back to work. Dr Hopkins had advised him to have some recuperation time before planning a gradual part-time return to work, she suggested not before November. Maybe there was pressure from his employers; I'm absolutely sure there was, as it was still September and Jon had already returned.

He was looking forward to it, and in preparation he had bought some smart new clothes and shoes. He had what remained of his now sparse hair cut short. His beard, which had not fallen out as expected during the treatment, was neatly trimmed into a trendy shadow. He sorted out bus times and was ready.

What a disappointment! It was not at all what he had imagined. He needed someone to rehabilitate him into the tasks required. The new benefit system for which he had been training was now up and running. He hadn't quite finished the training when he had had to stop, and anyway, there had inevitably been changes made as unforeseen complications came to light. But no one was available to help, so after a period of time, twiddling fingers and thumbs and trying to look busy, he made his own re-entry agenda, and tried to find his own way around the new systems.

Then came the next bombshell; a meeting was called to announce major changes. The Department at Fishponds was basically going to become a call centre. Prior to being rediagnosed, Jon had spent a lot of time on the telephone team. It was stressful; callers were often rude and abusive. Jon's head hurt just thinking about it. We will never know why Jon's tumour returned, but stress and the action of having a telephone to his ear for hours at a time couldn't be ruled out as a contributory factor.

Jon decided to apply for a transfer on medical grounds. Nobody questioned this, and before long he was offered an interview at Bath Job Centre Plus. He was impressed with that idea. He loved Bath, and felt that the work would really suit him. He enjoyed helping people. He knew how it felt to be unemployed and he felt that things were beginning to make sense.

The interview went well and he was offered the position. He was to start after Christmas. He was delighted and couldn't wait to begin his new role. It was great to have a genuine cause for celebrations!

Chapter Fifteen

JON MOVES TO BATH

January 2010

A cold and snowy start to the year presented transport problems straight away. Trains and buses to Bath were disrupted and cancelled. Somehow Jon battled through the freezing elements and managed to find his way there. The bad weather conditions had resulted in a depleted work force, so Jon was catapulted directly into customer contact. He learned on the job, and grew in confidence quickly. He had to work hard to meet the constraints of the time targets for each interview, but he really enjoyed the challenge and learnt quickly.

With a little help from Roy or me at this end meeting the train, he enjoyed the journey too. He loved being in Bath. It was a lively and vibrant place to be. During his lunch breaks he would explore his environs, and delighted in his surroundings. He felt very comfortable. He seemed well and happy and was coping well with being back at work.

In March he had a holiday. He had once again been invited to join the group of friends at the YCT house at Bournemouth. He was in good spirits as we delivered him to Temple Meads Station, where he met up with friends Bryony and Paul so that they could travel together on the train. He had a good week. Spending time with other young people that are going through similar circumstances, having the chance to be independent of your parents, and to enjoy special experiences with friends, is a valuable therapy. It was a unique place and he really benefited from this opportunity.

Soon after his return he started to complain of a stiff neck. He had carried a heavy rucksack to Bournemouth and I thought he had probably pulled a muscle. A lump appeared in his neck.

The following Sunday I became upset during a church service and retired to the vestry at the back, so that others wouldn't be aware of me crying. However, Joanne noticed that I was upset and came to join me. "What is it, Jacky?" she caringly enquired.

"Everything has just got too much at the moment," I admitted. "I'm worrying about Emily in New Zealand." She had come off her motorbike and had been in hospital with concussion. She seemed to be all right now, although there was a problem with her eye. "But now Jon has a lump in his neck," I continued. "I don't like lumps appearing!" We agreed that I was probably worrying unnecessarily, and Joanne gave me a hug.

Jon decided to go to the GP about the lump. "Most likely a virus," the doctor declared. "Nothing to worry about."

Just prior to his trip to Bournemouth, Jon had had a routine MRI scan. Now we had an appointment to see Dr Hopkins at the outpatients' clinic at Frenchay Hospital, for the results. Roy and I waited with Jon, anxiously anticipating the potentially exhilarating or devastating news. It was good! The scan was clear. There was no sign of the tumour.

Before we left, Jon mentioned the lump on his neck. She examined it. "I suppose you are thinking it might be the medulloblastoma having travelled down into your neck?" She had said what none of us had dared to voice. She looked at it again, "Nothing to worry about there, maybe a virus," she said. She did suggest, however, that should it still be there in a month, or if it grew any bigger, we should go back to the GP.

We left the consulting room in a state of jubilation. Jon had requested that if the news was good, we should go to the Brimsham for dinner. There was every reason to celebrate and we enjoyed a hearty pub meal together.

During the evening Jon discussed plans to look for a flat to rent in Bath. He felt reassured by his visit to Dr Hopkins and thought it would be a good step forward. The travelling times to Bath made his working day long, and the thought of moving into his own place really excited him.

Jon and I spent the following Sunday afternoon touring the various different areas of Bath, finding out about the different locations. We were soon able to discern the pleasant places from the rough areas, the peaceful from the rowdy.

The following week we visited a few properties that had been advertised on the internet. Mostly they were quite scruffy and very expensive. One place kept popping up on the search. It wasn't what Jon was looking for as it was a bedsit, so it was ignored. However, it persisted in popping up, so on one visit we went to see where it was located. We discovered that it was on a fine Georgian Street, close to Royal Crescent and The Victoria Park. Jon decided it was worth a look.

When we arrived we were initially put off as we discovered that it was a basement, with a flight of stone steps. That was quite a negative for Jon, he wasn't keen on steps. But then we were shown inside.

It was gorgeous! The newly-decorated bed-sitting room was huge, with great big windows looking out at pavement level. We then were shown the huge kitchen, well equipped with a homely pine kitchen table and chairs, a dishwasher and the central heating boiler. French windows looked out onto a tiny patio area too, at the foot of steps going up to the garden. A long hallway led to a quirky, cellar-like shower room. It was all freshly painted, clean and white. The utility bills were all included in the price too. It was super. "Yes please!" said an enthusiastic and excited Jon.

Jon moved in on May 1st 2010. He took a few days' leave from work, and had a wonderful time arranging his furniture and belongings. The flat was part-furnished, so Jon brought along his own bed and wardrobe. He chose a settee, armchair and rug to create a sitting end to the room, where his television, CD player and coffee table were also to live. Shopping trips to buy exciting things like cutlery and a dinner service from Habitat gave him enormous pleasure. He bought new bright red bedding and I crocheted for all I was worth to make a red and brown throw for his new settee.

The walk to work was a real pleasure. On his way to work he saw tourists from Japan, America, and other countries photographing landmarks such as Queen's Square and Royal Crescent. He couldn't believe his luck to live in such a special place.

He didn't neglect God either. He worshipped at various churches in the vicinity and even attended an evening service at Bath Abbey. He was counting his blessings, and thanking God for his good fortune. We all were.

Across the road from the flat was a GP practice. As he continued to need regular three-weekly injections, he decided to sign on there as a new patient.

Around the same time Jon had been appointed Finance Officer at work. He was flattered to have been given this responsibility and worked very hard to do a good job. His hours started to increase enormously as he attempted to keep up with this demanding work, and inevitably his stress levels increased. It couldn't have come at a worse time as he had also taken on the responsibility of his own home, with all that that entailed.

Then the lump in his neck started to become a problem. It grew and was painful, and the whole area around it became inflamed. He visited his new GP's surgery. Jon was of the opinion that it was an infection, and certainly the redness and pain suggested that to me too. But the doctor he saw alarmed him, and thought it could be a tumour. Jon now waited anxiously for a hospital referral.

The ENT department at Bath Royal United Hospital sent for him. The first doctor he saw performed a syringe test, but the results proved inconclusive. We felt that this was a good sign, as no cancer was showing.

The hospital doctor now decided that a biopsy was required. It was a painful period, and time moved slowly.

Eventually the day arrived for the biopsy, at the Royal United Hospital. The surgeon came to see him afterwards and was sympathetic. "It doesn't look sinister, nothing to worry about," he suggested to the now sore and weary Jon.

"Whew!" We were all so relieved. Jon recovered from the biopsy quite quickly, although his neck was still sore, but not enough to stop him enjoying the St. Mary's Church Flower Festival which followed. Our minds were taken off the biopsy and we threw ourselves into the many activities at the festival. I was responsible for the catering, so I had a lot to do and Jon was a good help as always. We were well distracted.

The follow-up appointment for the results of the biopsy was on the Monday after the flower festival. It was a fine July day. We all went in to see the doctor.

Without any preamble the doctor stated baldly, "It's medulloblastoma."

There was a stunned silence. None of us could take in the enormity of this statement. We had been so reassured by so many different people. Jon refused to believe it. The doctor was about to refer us to the Bath Oncology Department. "Hang on!" said Jon, "I have an oncologist already in Bristol, can't I see her?"

The doctor readily agreed to allow Jon to make his own arrangements to see Dr Hopkins. That was easier said than done, however. Jon spent the next hour frantically trying to make contact with her or her secretary, or the department, on his mobile phone. We sat on a wall in the car park of the Bath hospital, attempting to be calm. But like the legs of ducks gliding on the water's surface, our minds were going crazily underneath.

When eventually Jon got through, they didn't seem to suggest any urgency. There were more tissue tests to be done on the biopsy sample. They would contact us with an appointment date within the next week.

Jon refused to believe this diagnosis. Until he heard it from Dr Hopkins, he would NOT believe them!

Jon had moved back home again, his recently-furbished flat abandoned. He was morose about it. He remembered how it felt to have just moved into the flat in Greenways, only to move out again. "It's happening again!" he said sadly. He refused to empty the fridge. He believed he would be going back. However he did let his work know that he wouldn't be in for the time being. He was signed off sick.

We decided to lift our spirits by having a few days away at Malvern with the caravan. Two things happened then which should have made us change our plans. The appointment to see Dr Hopkins was made for the Wednesday of that week, and Dave, Jon's boss and the Job Centre manager, made arrangements to call to see him. We decided that as Malvern was only an hour away, we could still go and travel back for these two occasions.

Coming back to meet up with Dave was like a farcical play. Jon didn't want to admit that we were taking a break – in his mind it seemed the wrong thing to be doing if you were signed off sick. So we came back to the house and attempted to appear that we were living there and doing normal things, when in fact we were just waiting for him to go, so that we could return to Malvern and have our dinner. I don't know if he saw through our charade, it really doesn't matter now at all.

The other appointment was rather different. We made our way to Frenchay Outpatients for the meeting with Dr Hopkins. We were all clinging to the idea that it was all a big mistake. It wasn't. Dr Hopkins, in her very quiet voice, told us the bad news. "I'm afraid Jon, that this is a very serious development," she said. The specialist nurse Lois was there too and she was very kind and suitably sympathetic.

Many other tests were to follow. The cancer, having reached the lymph glands, could have travelled anywhere in the body. It would have to be established just where it had reached.

We made our sombre and tearful way back to Malvern. I suggested that we should pack up our caravan and head for home. "No!" said Jon firmly, "we may as well stay for the remaining couple of days, it won't be any different at home." Jon retired to his awning bedroom on our return, alone with his thoughts.

The following day we climbed up and walked along the Malvern Hills. We sat on a summit, looking over the views in quiet contemplation of the rocky journey ahead. I prayed that God would give us the strength to endure what was coming.

All manner of tests had to be endured. The bone marrow test, even under sedation, was nightmarishly painful. Jon was so brave. The tests revealed that the cancer was in the brain, but thankfully nowhere else in the body.

Dr Hopkins now suggested a course of chemotherapy: a cocktail of Irinotechin and Temozolomide. Apparently this had been used before somewhere in the world, with good results. It did, however, require Jon to go into the Oncology Centre's Chemotherapy Day Unit, every weekday for three weeks. Then he could have a week off, and then start all over again for a probable six cycles. We were horrified at the prospect of going into the hospital *every day*!

Jon, as ever, accepted the situation without hesitation. "If that's what it takes, that's what I'll do!" he said. It was scheduled to start in the last week in August.

For the first week, the chemotherapy was administered through a needle into a vein in the back of his hand. As the week went on, it became increasingly difficult. Despite bowls of warm water, and attempts by a number of nurses, they all failed to find the elusive veins. Something had to be done. Although initially resistant to the idea, Jon agreed that a PICC line (peripherally inserted central catheter) in his arm would make the process a lot easier. It was scheduled for the following week.

Chapter Sixteen

GREENBELT 2010

It was the last weekend in August, a bank holiday, and the weekend of the Greenbelt Festival. We hadn't considered going, but Jon was very enthusiastic. We wondered how we could do this, given the commitment of the treatment programme. We made a plan of action.

Roy set off alone early on the Friday morning, with the caravan, in order to get a good spot on the caravan site and to set everything up. Jon's chemo appointment was mid-morning. He was eager to go on to Greenbelt from there. The slow dripping of the potent chemicals into Jon's vein seemed to take forever, much longer than usual. Eventually it was in, the flush was done and we were free to go. Excitedly, we set off for the drive to Cheltenham; Jon made himself comfortable for a sleep on the back seat of my car on the way.

How wonderful it was to arrive to find our accommodation all set up and waiting for us. Roy had done a splendid job putting up the awning alone; everything looked great. It was a very good arrangement!

Despite his enthusiasm, Jon wasn't up to doing much really. He was very weary and a bit queasy. He was determined to enjoy as much as he was able though. We spent some time in the 'performance café' during the day and listened to the main stage music from inside the caravan in the evening. He was glad to be there.

Inside my head, away from my cheerful front, I was screaming. Would this be our last Greenbelt? Would Jon still be alive in a year's time? I followed a sign advertising a Greenbelt counsellor: 'Come in for a chat with one of our counsellors' it invited. The pleasant middle-aged man welcomed me in, but as I started to relate my worries, I could see that he was out of his depth and he struggled to find a suitable response. There were no right words. At least it helped me to voice my concerns.

The treatment, now with PICC line in place, continued throughout the autumn. Jon was a familiar face now at the Oncology Centre and everyone, from the lady on the reception desk, to the nurses in the chemotherapy day unit, knew his name. "Hi Jon!" they would call. It was friendly and we felt oddly at home.

Jon was delighted to be back in the fold of the family of St. Mary's Church. He now seemed to be a very popular young man. He had been involved in several of the house groups and lots of church events and people liked his warmth and caring nature. They wanted to show that they cared about him, so a dynamic group set about organising a special night. They included him in the planning and a disco was decided upon, with a promises auction. They intended to give Jon the proceeds from the evening, but there was no way he would accept that, so it was agreed to donate the money raised to Jon's chosen charity, CLIC Sargent, the charity that had helped him so much during his initial year of treatment.

The event was a great success. Jon found the necessary energy and rose to the occasion. The first lovely surprise was being collected in a limousine. It was a very smart way to arrive at an evening planned especially for him. The disco took place in St. Mary's Youth Centre and it had been transformed with lights, decorations and balloons. A bar was in place, selling, among other things, Jon's drink of choice – cider.

The disco was lively and the music was exciting and good for dancing. There was also a guitarist playing folksy music which added to the atmosphere. Jon's grin was wide with delight when Heather appeared with one of his favourite things; a huge chocolate cake, white chocolate buttons spelling out JON. His smile lit up the room. Next was the promises auction. So many people had donated their time, energy and skills and each lot had plenty of interested bidders. They ranged from an hour's ironing to a bottle of House of Commons red wine. All in all the evening raised a magnificent £2000. Jon had the most special of evenings. He went to bed at last, completely exhausted but extremely pleased with himself.

The following Sunday, he was surprised again when he was presented with some gifts: a voucher to buy a fish tank and an aquarium book, tickets for the SS *Great Britain* and a meal at the Swan in the nearby village of Nibley. All were things that he had been talking about. He was thrilled. It was also very special to be able to present an oversized cheque to a representative of the CLIC Sargent charity.

I realise that I haven't mentioned Jon's hut yet, or what happened to his flat. Very reluctantly, and with great sadness, he gave up his flat. He considered staying there, but he had stopped work, he needed to get into Bristol for treatment, and more than anything else he needed our loving company. He was happy to be back at home, and back in the friendliness of Yate, but disappointed that his stay in Bath had been so short lived.

On one journey across to Bath he talked about his sadness. "Would you rather have never lived in Bath at all?" I asked.

"No", he replied, "I'm so glad that I had that experience, glad that I got to know Bath, even if it wasn't long enough."

The new furniture he had bought for his flat was now sitting unused in our garage. It was sad to see it. Suddenly I came up with the idea of creating Jon's own space. We had looked in the past at those lovely wooden summer houses and admired them, and now we thought that maybe one would fit in our garden, a hut for Jon. Early in September, in pouring rain, an expert team of strapping men erected his log cabin in our garden. We had electricity and Sky TV installed and set about recreating Jon's living room from the flat. He was delighted. It was smart and warm and cosy. It was a place of his own, to entertain friends or just chill out with a movie. He bought a wooden kitchen trolley in which to keep his new crockery, and he stocked it with tea and sugar, hot chocolate powder and biscuits. He was as independent as he wanted to be. It also had the advantage over the Bath flat in that it was at ground level and the sun poured into his open doors. He could sit and look out onto the garden. He could breathe in the tranquillity of this peaceful and beautiful place.

Towards the end of October, Jon had been having treatment for nearly two months. The lump in his neck had disappeared and he was feeling well enough to take full advantage of a week off chemo. He filled the week with outings with friends, trips to the pub and quiz nights.

At the end of the week we decided to use our SS *Great Britain* tickets, so we set off for Bristol. It was a special fun day and Jon and Roy played around together, trying on Isambard's high hat and teasing one another.

Although it's October, it is a mild day and Jon is hot. At lunchtime he takes off his jumper. His tee shirt is soaking wet. "It's not *that* hot!" I declare.

As soon as we arrive home I find the thermometer. His temperature is way up higher than normal. I ring the Oncology Centre. "Bring him straight in!" they instruct. As we drive into Bristol for the second time that day, Jon jokes about taking me 'out on the town' on a Friday night. He puts a comment on Facebook about the great view from his hospital window, high up on the third floor.

Over the weekend his temperature returns to normal, and on Monday, after many inconclusive blood tests, he is allowed to come home again. He is delighted, "The food at the weekend in the Oncology Centre is not much like home cooking!" he observes.

The next morning, as he appears for breakfast, I notice that he is very flushed. I take his temperature; it is high again. I expect the Oncology Centre will tell us to come back, but surprisingly they don't. "Go to Accident and Emergency at Frenchay Hospital," they say. They explain that all their beds are allocated.

At Frenchay, Jon endures all the same blood tests over again. They discover that his oxygen levels are low, and supply him with an oxygen tube, to put up his nose. We are in a cubicle, awaiting a decision, for hours. I realise that the car park time will soon expire, so I set about finding enough change to purchase another ticket. I buy a drink and a sandwich from the cafeteria to get some more cash. I put it all in the machine, every penny. I am relieved that I won't have to think about it again for the rest of the day.

I return to Jon in his cubicle. Suddenly paramedics arrive. "We've come to take you to Southmead," they announce.

"What?" Jon and I cry in unison. "No one has mentioned anything about Southmead."

I watch them shut the ambulance doors and drive away, then I collapse in tears. I am at the end of my tether, and now Jon has gone from me all the emotion and worry come hurtling to the surface and spill over. Southmead Hospital is new territory; we are familiar with Frenchay. A great fear of the unknown engulfs me.

A kind nurse takes me in hand. I explain how I have *just* put all my money into the car park machine. I won't be able to park at Southmead. She rings through to the hospital and clears it for me to be able to park there without incurring a fine. They just need my registration number. I ring Roy and tell him what has happened. He makes his way there too.

We catch up with Jon in the admissions ward. Nothing really has happened yet, but when a doctor does come to see him, he explains how they will need to take various blood tests. We question the lack of communication between hospitals – surely they could get the results from the tests that he has already had? Apparently not. They do quickly supply him with some oxygen.

After a couple of days, he is moved to the respiratory ward. This seems to have been the plan all along, but it wasn't clear to us. His oxygen levels are plummeting; x-rays are showing pneumonia in both lungs. He is deteriorating fast.

During a morning phone conversation with the doctor on the ward, it is suggested that it would be okay for us to come and be with him, out of visiting hours! We waste no time in getting there.

The doctor from the intensive care unit comes to examine Jon. At another time he would have admitted him, but as there is a case of swine flu there they decide to leave Jon on the ward, under constant surveillance.

By now Jon has been fitted with a CPAP machine (Continuous Positive Airway Pressure). We are warned before we enter the ward. It looks very frightening. The machine is breathing for him and Jon is relying on it for nearly all his oxygen. As it covers his face he can't eat, so a nasogastric tube is fitted. He can't really speak either, so we just sit by his bed and hold his hand.

Evening comes and it is time for us to leave the ward. Jon looks at me very deliberately; I lean in towards him to give him a kiss. "Goodbye," he whispers.

Miraculously, and it really was a miracle, an answer to the many fervent prayers that were being said for him, Jon started to recover. His oxygen levels started to rise; the CPAP's use was gradually reduced. Jon started to be able to eat, and to speak. Soon we were playing Scrabble. We said our grateful prayers of thanks.

Jon was desperate to leave the hospital. His oxygen levels were restored to normal, apart from, puzzlingly, during the night, when they dropped dramatically. Until they were steady Jon wasn't allowed to come home. Tests revealed that on several occasions during the night, Jon had stopped breathing all together. The nurses teased him "You forgot to breathe, Jon!" Sleep apnoea was diagnosed. This being established, he now had to wait for a breathing pump to be delivered. He would need to use this to keep his oxygen levels up whilst he was sleeping. Unfortunately, the supplier of breathing pumps was based at the sleep clinic at Bristol General Hospital in Guinea Street. They shut at weekends of course, so Jon had to wait until the following week. He was very frustrated.

Eventually the big ugly thing arrived, and after instruction in its use and care, Jon was finally able to come home. He had been in hospital for more than two weeks and now it was mid-November. The weather had turned from the mild and pleasant autumn to a bitter cold winter. Jon didn't like being fussed, but we warned him before he came home that he might just have to get used to being wrapped in at least a smidgeon of cotton wool for now! He laughingly accepted the truth of this. It had been a close shave and he didn't want to repeat it.

His lovely hut was now abandoned for the winter. It didn't seem to make sense to recover from double pneumonia, then to go outside in the cold to sit in what could be described as a shed! Jon's plans for Christmas decorations for his hut were shelved.

Jon had to get used to sleeping with a pump by his side and a mask on his face. It took a bit of getting used to. Sleep clinic appointments and more tests now had to be added to our already busy programme.

It was thought that singing might be good lung exercise, so a hunt for a singing teacher was started. Nurse Lois was wonderfully supportive and she applied for a grant from CLIC Sargent to help to pay for a course of singing lessons. An internet search found a number of possible teachers, but Jane, based in Chipping Sodbury, was the favourite. We went to meet her in her pretty cottage. Jon and Jane seemed to get on very well. He loved going along for his singing and when the course was coming to an end, he eagerly signed up for the next one. I think they shared a similar quirky sense of humour; she must have made him relax, as he was very shy of singing in front of people.

Jon continued his singing lessons with enthusiasm, and a good friendship developed between him and Jane. He was keen to choose the songs that he was singing and bought several sheet music books to take along. A favourite song that they returned to over and over again was *Hallelujah*. Later on Jane had bought Jon a cap with the words *Bring Me Sunshine* embroidered on the front, another favourite, and a cheerful song. He never performed his songs at home, but I did notice that when singing hymns in church, he had a confidence that hadn't been there before.

Chapter Seventeen

A SURPRISE VISIT, AND MORE SURGERY

After the scare of pneumonia, Jon was now extra vigilant at avoiding germs. His standards of hygiene had always been high, but now they were exceptional. He managed to keep sufficiently well to continue the chemotherapy regime without interruption.

Jon's birthday and Christmas were approaching when I noticed a competition in the *Evening Post*. A special Christmas visit from one of the Bristol football teams was being offered to a deserving recipient. Jon was an avid follower of Bristol Rovers. He had often been to home games with his friend Stephen, and kept up with their progress. So I decided to have a go. I wrote my story about 'Pirate' Jon, telling them of his condition and how he was now having to have chemotherapy every day (including his birthday). I was so thrilled when I received an email to say that my letter had done the trick, they had chosen Jon to be the winner.

As Jon was spending so much time at the Oncology Centre, I suggested that it might be appropriate to visit him there. I thought the nurses would enjoy it too. It was so exciting, as Jon knew nothing about it at all. I was bursting to tell him. I had warned the reception staff and some of the nurses, so there was an air of anticipation in the unit. Then I had a moment of anxiety, I hoped that Jon wouldn't be embarrassed, I hoped that he wouldn't be cross with me, I hoped that he'd know who his visitors were!

I am glad to say that I needn't have worried. Jon was thrilled! He was delighted to meet one of his heroes, striker Will Hoskins, and of course he knew exactly who he was. Will came with an entourage of other players and some *Evening Post* reporters. They filled the chemotherapy day unit and it raised the spirits of everyone who was there. Jon chatted knowledgeably about the team and how they were doing, and joked about applying for the manager's job!

Will came bearing gifts too, a signed shirt and football and a photo of the team. These were to become cherished possessions, along with the photographs that were taken and especially the one that was in the newspaper write-up. Will Hoskins, being the same age as Jon, had learned something as well. He told me that he had never been anywhere like that before, he had not known that whilst he was busy making a career out of playing football, others were enduring the pain of debilitating treatment, with all the accompanying worry. He was suitably humbled by this eye-opening visit.

January 2011

After Christmas the chemotherapy regime changed; Jon was no longer required to attend every day. It was now reduced to once a week, but the dosage had been increased enormously. Whilst Jon had just about coped with the effects of the chemo before, now this high dose knocked him for six. He slept a lot and rested in between. He wasn't really up to doing very much at all.

His perseverance was rewarded, however, as in late February his scan results were completely clear. Dr Hopkins and Nurse Toni were jumping up and down with delight.

"You are a star, Jon!" Dr Hopkins declared triumphantly, "Well done!" She suggested that we took a holiday. We set off for home with elation. Definitely an evening for dinner at the pub!

We didn't realise how urgent that holiday was. It was February and chilly. After lots of research and discussion we booked a 'Freedom of France' holiday in Brittany for early June. Jon thought it would recreate some of our early family holidays and he was very enthusiastic about that.

The medulloblastoma had other ideas. By Jon's next scan in April, it was back. We were told the news in early May. We were devastated. The roller-coaster that goes up comes down again with such force.

Dr Hopkins put on her quiet voice again to break the bad news. She seemed to really feel for Jon. He had battled through months of heavy chemo, and here it was, so soon, back again. She felt she needed to have something to offer Jon now. She had spoken already to Mr Porter, the surgeon, and his team. They had agreed to more surgery. We were surprised; could they really do the same operation a third time?

The risks were greater and the surgery would be more aggressive. Jon had the choice; he could decline the offer. But this is Jon we are talking about. "I'm not giving up!" he stated decisively. The surgery was planned. The holiday was cancelled.

Whilst waiting for the day of surgery to come around, we took every opportunity to have some outings. Most memorable was a beautiful day at Weston-Super-Mare. The sun shone and we enjoyed each other's company – on the train, on the big wheel, on the beach, on the pier and eating fish and chips. It was a truly golden day.

The day of Jon's surgery was not a golden day. He was admitted into Ward 19, one of the old and crumbling wards, across the road from the main building. He had to arrive the day before the surgery. It was pouring with rain and we were very low in spirits. Back at home in the evening, I left a telephone message for a hospital chaplain, asking if they would visit Jon. I thought it might help and I was searching for ideas of practical things to do. I also emailed Hammer Out and asked for their support.

Jon's operation was scheduled for 11am. He was gowned and sitting on his curtained bed. On the dot of eleven, the curtains pulled back to reveal a lovely lady chaplain. She was just what Jon needed. She held his hands and prayed with us. There was a moment of calm. Seconds later the porters came to wheel him on a trolley to theatre.

You have to cross the road to get to the theatres. It was still pouring with rain. I thought he'd get soaked on the way across. As we left the ward, the rain suddenly abated, the sun appeared from behind a cloud and shone for the briefest of moments. I just knew that God was with us.

It was a long day, and Roy and I decided to go home. We couldn't face another endless day of waiting around at the hospital. We'd been here twice before. We were told that we wouldn't be able to see Jon after the surgery anyway as he would still be in recovery when visiting time was over. We were in close contact by phone however, and we did return to the hospital as soon as we heard that the surgery had been successful. He was still on the recovery ward and was being kept there as he was being rather sick. We were not allowed to see him.

We went in again first thing in the morning. He looked dreadful. He was bloodied and bruised and it hurt him to move. We didn't stay for long, and after a kiss we left him to sleep, promising to return for the afternoon visiting time.

In the meantime, Rachel had arrived. She had taken some time off work and had driven down to be with us. We went in to see Jon together. What a transformation! He was almost unrecognisable from the wreck of the morning. He was washed, dressed and sitting in a chair eating a meal. We were amazed and incredulous that he could have bounced back so quickly. He was also thrilled to show us a text message that he had received from Beth Rowley, wishing him well after his operation. She was another favourite of his, a singer-songwriter who we had seen perform at Greenbelt. She was also a patron of Hammer Out. How his spirits were raised by that message of support.

The surgery had been aggressive though, and he did take longer to recover this time. During the icy winter Jon had started to use a stick to steady himself on slippery ground. Now he used it all the time and was glad of it. He was wobbly and often felt he might fall. He was very easily fatigued and was always ready for a sleep. But with rest and the prayers of our friends, he began to gather strength again and had a renewed appetite for life.

He had continued to have counselling sessions with Kate through Hammer Out, but lately he had been going to their meetings at Thornbury as well. Sometimes I went with him. Shortly after his surgery I went along, and as he hadn't mentioned it, I eventually told everyone how Jon had recently come through a third lot of brain surgery. They were all amazed and said that they would never have guessed, as he looked so well. He didn't dwell on his own problems, but never failed to enquire about the wellbeing of others. Julie, a 'Hammer Out' friend, and the wife of Steve, another brain tumour patient, remarked that Jon always answered the question "How are you?" with the same question, asked right back.

Summer 2011

We had booked to spend a night in a hotel in Portsmouth, en route to our holiday in France. Of course we had cancelled that as well, but when I explained the situation to the manager, he offered to defer our stay with them until Jon felt well enough.

So it was that we set off for a couple of days in Portsmouth. Jon probably wasn't really well enough, but he had great enthusiasm and enjoyed this city break. We were sitting on a bench, waiting for the boat trip round Portsmouth Historic Harbour, when we realised people were noticing Jon's hat. It was the hat that Jane had bought him, the golden letters declaring 'BRING ME SUNSHINE!' It was a very apt slogan on a cool and breezy day. It was also in Portsmouth that he bought himself another iconic hat. It was a warm pull-on beanie embroidered with the words 'KNACKERED SAILOR'. He felt this slogan summed him up at the time.

Jon amazed us by joining us on an 'uplifting' trip to the top of the Spinnaker Tower. Considering his fear of heights, we were very impressed by his determination and bravery. It wasn't quite the French holiday we had planned, but we all felt the benefit of the change of scenery, the fresh air and exercise.

Now we had another appointment with Dr Hopkins, who prescribed more chemotherapy. This time it was in the form of tablets that he could take at home. It was also expected to be less debilitating than some of the other drugs Jon had taken in the past. Nevertheless, on Jon's much-treated body, the side effects took their toll.

We had another little holiday. This time we went to Lynmouth in Devon. It was a beautiful spot and we loved the position of the Rock House Hotel, which was right by the sea, with wonderful views from the bedroom windows. The weather was cool for July, but it didn't stop us having a pleasant few days enjoying one another's company and the invigorating sea air. Jon loved us being together in this way. Perhaps we were clinging on to his presence, aware that he would not always be around. He was so tired. He slept so readily, having an afternoon sleep and an early night each day.

We set off to visit Lee Abbey, just minutes from Lynmouth. Jon had booked himself into a church weekend there the previous September. His demanding chemotherapy regime had put paid to that, so we thought we would go along to visit. Within moments of starting the car engine, Jon was fast asleep. Roy and I appreciated the beautiful setting of this spiritual place, but we could only describe it to Jon.

We hadn't considered going to Greenbelt. It didn't seem at all likely that we would even think about it, but one sunny afternoon, sitting in the garden, the subject came up.

"No I don't think so, not this year," I remarked. Jon was not up to the rigours of caravanning and walking round all day. Not well enough at all.

"Well" Jon said emphatically, "I'm going anyway. Whether you're going or not!" We all laughed, it seemed preposterous. But it did the trick, we bought tickets!

Miraculously, and most surprisingly, the caravan site still

had a grass pitch available. (These are usually all booked up by January.)

I noticed in the advertising literature that there was a hire company loaning out mobility scooters, the first time they had been at the festival. I mentioned it to Jon, but he was very unenthusiastic and understandably negative. I suggested that he gave one a try at Westonbirt Arboretum, where you could borrow one for free, and he agreed. As his confidence grew, he grinned, and then shot away into the distance, leaving us standing! He decided that, after all, it would be great to have one at Greenbelt.

The sleeping arrangements at Greenbelt were turned on their heads too. Usually Roy and I slept in the caravan and Jon had his own awning extension bedroom. This year we decided that Jon needed the proper bed, the electricity connection for his breathing pump and the proximity to the caravan bathroom. It amused him no end to see us crawling into our 'tent' bedroom! He made us laugh too with his 'Lord of the Manor' impressions.

It was a good Greenbelt. The scooter opened up events for Jon that he would never have reached on foot. He negotiated the crowds, the bumps and the hills with aplomb. Having the scooter also meant that we got to see Folk On. Reading about them in the programme, they sounded right up Jon's street, but when we arrived at the Performance Café it was clear that other people liked the sound of them too. It was packed! Fortunately, there was an area to one side of the stage that was reserved for disabled people, and Jon and his scooter were ushered down to the front. I was able to accompany him, and found a bit of grassy ground to sit on, just beside him.

Folk On did not disappoint. We laughed, and laughed, and laughed some more. They sang about things close to Jon's heart, like solving the world's problems with hugs. They sang about surprising things too, like a pet slug, and a dead horse, and Jon loved it.

I don't know if we knew that this would be Jon's last Greenbelt. Perhaps we had stopped thinking like that.

Within hours of returning home, Jon had researched mobility scooters. Three days later he had bought his own. He was incredibly proud of it. It was a smart silver and black one, tidy and streamlined. Jon took control of it at once and discovered a sense of freedom and independence that he had almost forgotten had once existed. He was fearless and confident and took himself off to Yate, to church and the shops, and even as far as Chipping Sodbury, sometimes just whizzing around for the sheer pleasure of getting around unaided.

On the reverse of the scooter were the initials 'TGA'. Without any hesitation, 'Tigger' became the scooter's name. Jon's good friend Dawn encouraged this personalisation by buying him a pocket-sized Disney

Tigger to go in the basket. A Tigger-sized Bristol Rovers hat and scarf were soon to follow.

Sadly there were a few negative comments about 'looking like an old man', but Jon shrugged them off. The benefits were too good, and far outweighed any negativity.

Autumn 2011

Rachel's wedding plans were gathering speed and Jon was not enthusiastic about it at all. He grumbled about the female preoccupation with dresses, flowers, colour schemes and the like. I think he was secretly very sad that it wasn't his wedding, and realised that was unlikely to ever happen. He was, however, very happy to have been asked to be an usher. He delighted in his grey morning suit and ivory waistcoat. He enjoyed buying himself 'ROCK STAR' cuff links and had a secret plan to wear a pair of very bright pink socks, as a token contribution to the colour scheme!

September came and brought the arrival of Emily and Bruce. He was happy and distracted by their company. He spent a particularly fun day in Bristol with Bruce, photographing the decorated gorillas that adorned the city at that time, whilst Emily and I had much less fun, attempting to buy bridesmaids' shoes.

A hot sunny Sunday was the day of the Bristol Half Marathon. Emily had entered and was running in aid of

Hammer Out, the brain tumour charity that had given Jon so much support. It was exciting to share the buzz of anticipation in Bristol that day. Emily was raring to go, with a spring in her step and a wide smile as she was waiting for the signal to start. Off she went and we meanwhile crossed Bristol to the various points where we might see her as the route passed by. Jon perhaps should not have come, or maybe we should have brought his scooter with us. He was exhausted and grey, and found the walking round Bristol far too strenuous. It was a reminder to us all that although he looked quite well, and people often remarked on it, he really wasn't nearly as strong as he appeared.

The September trip to Bournemouth YCT was upon us, and we delivered Jon to Temple Meads Station to meet up with Bryony and Paul. He was anxious about a proposed sailing trip to the Isle of Wight. He knew he was not up to it. Even just getting onto the boat was a worry. We discussed it before he went; he could decline, he was not obliged to participate in this activity. He resolved to stay back at the house on that day. But he didn't. He sailed to the Isle of Wight! He was hugely proud of himself, and photographs of the occasion show a beaming and confident Jon, steering the boat. In reality he was feeling pretty queasy and now could lay proper claim to the slogan on his hat. A truly 'KNACKERED SAILOR'.

Chapter Eighteen

A WEDDING
AND A HOLIDAY

October 8th 2011

The weekend of Rachel's wedding at last arrived and we all set off in a two-car convoy. Jon and I led the way, Jon keeping a watchful eye in the wing mirror to check that Roy, Emily and Bruce weren't too far behind. We decided we needed two cars as we had rather a lot of important luggage. Special clothes and a large hat box, speeches, poems and bunting and five people take up quite a bit of space!

The previous weekend had been gloriously warm with real Indian summer weather, so it was disappointing that we arrived in torrential rain. Great lake-sized puddles surrounded the hotel, but our spirits were not dampened. We were all allocated last-minute jobs, attaching ribbons to service booklets and filling bags with rose petal confetti.

Jon was allocated a small but adequate ground floor hotel room, and took the opportunity to have an afternoon sleep. We, meanwhile, moved the newly-collected wedding dress into our palatial executive suite, where it hung gloriously with the train draped carefully across the floor. We then delivered the many clearly-labelled boxes to another room in the hotel, ready for use the next day. A relaxed and pleasant family meal rounded off the eve of the wedding.

The wedding day dawned – dry, at least. Our room was requisitioned as a girls' preparation room, and soon it was filled with an atmosphere of calm excitement as the hairdresser and make-up artist began their craft. The florist arrived with beautiful floral arrangements, bouquets and corsages. A bottle of bubbly and a silver tray of sparkling flutes arrived as a gift from the groom.

Meanwhile our men prepared themselves in Bruce's room. Jon was hugely proud of his scrubbed-up-self and posed for photographs. He looked wonderful, and felt good too. All his grumpiness about the wedding had evaporated and he set about having a great day, being the proud brother of the bride and an usher amongst the groom's men. He thoroughly enjoyed the occasion, the food and drink, meeting and chatting with family and friends. He amazed us all by staying the course and it was gone eleven o'clock when he collapsed exhausted into bed.

It was a miraculous and welcome blessing that Jon was

able to share so fully in Rachel and Neill's very special day.

At our request, Jon's October MRI scan had been delayed until after the wedding. We didn't want to run the risk of having either a negative result, or the anxious wait for the result hanging over us on the joyous occasion. So it was a huge relief and cause for celebration when the scan results were clear. We cheered for joy and there were smiles all around the consulting room. "I think you need a break from chemo now," said Dr Hopkins. "Have three months off, and we'll review the situation in February."

Jon straight away started to plan his travelling, sharing ideas with Dawn, who encouraged him, buying him a *Rough Guide to Britain* and maps of the UK. He knew he would not get insurance to travel abroad, and wasn't really up to that anyway, so he planned something closer to home. He decided he would travel to the extremities of the country, visiting the most southerly, northerly, easterly and westerly points of the Great British Isles.

The opportunity to visit the most westerly point (of Wales) came pretty quickly. Jon was a regular reader of the *Bristol Evening Post*. Early in November they ran a competition to win a holiday in Pembrokeshire. Jon and I both entered the competition, but it was Jon who got the phone call.

"Hi, this is the Evening Post," he was told. "You've won a holiday at Bluestone in Pembrokeshire!"

"Wahoo!" shouted Jon in response. He teased us about who he might take on holiday with him. Happily he chose to take his dad and me. A double celebration, as it was also a special treat for Roy's birthday at the end of the month.

What a day! As we arrived the black skies were throwing down torrents of rain. It was blowing horizontally in great sheets, illuminated in our car headlights. Searching through the dark park, we eventually found our log cabin. Putting the key into the door, we were not sure what we were going to find. We were not disappointed. It was cosy and warm and beautifully furnished. It was stylish and very comfortable. Jon was particularly impressed with his bedroom. It was equipped with a very upmarket en-suite bathroom with walk-in wet room, warmed with underfloor heating. Jon was in his element.

During this week we were also able to visit Jon's beloved St. David's, his westerly moment! We drove down the lane to St. Non's and then waited for a gap in the rain showers. We watched the rain coming in great waves across the stormy sea. Briefly the rain abated, so hurriedly we made our way down across the wet and slippery grass to St. Non's Well, our place of pilgrimage. As on previous occasions, we anointed Jon's troubled head with the Holy Water from the healing well, and said our prayers of thanks.

The weather gradually improved and we had a wonderful week. We were all in such good spirits and really enjoyed the facilities of the park. The water park, with its warm water, fabulous wave machine and lazy river, was a great place to relax and have some fun. Most evenings we strolled down the hill to the Village Pub, cheerfully anticipating a tasty dinner to come.

There was the first hint of Christmas too. We watched as the park began to put up the festive Christmas lights, and children dressed as little Santa's elves started to appear amongst the family groups.

Seaside places in winter have a special magic somehow, and Tenby was no exception. We enjoyed a beautiful day there and Jon returned with a tiny but beautifully carved nativity set, created from a section of log.

The Christmas period had still more treats in store. Way back in August Nurse Lois had suggested Jon should apply for a 'Special Day' with the Willow Foundation. This is a charity set up by Bob Wilson and his wife in memory of their daughter. It provides seriously ill young people with a special experience. As we had not heard from them by December, we had forgotten all about it. So it was a great surprise when suddenly it was on!

Jon had requested a trip to London. He particularly wanted to see *Mamma Mia*; he knew it would be cheerful and fun. So here we were, mid-December and on a train to London. In true style we were met by a taxi that transported us across London to a fabulous luxury hotel overlooking the Thames, our accommodation for the night. It was in a very central London location and we meandered along the streets of Westminster drinking in the grandeur of the historic buildings. We found a lively pub serving wholesome tasty food, and we were glad to sit down and enjoy each other's company over a meal. We returned to the hotel to get ready for our special evening. Soon enough a taxi arrived to whisk us off to the theatre. What a super fun and happy evening! We all enjoyed it so much, singing along and cheering with enthusiasm.

The following morning was as bright and clear as could be for mid-December. After a splendid breakfast we made our way to the London Eye, a ten-minute walk along the Albert Embankment. We were in place to be the first customers of the day! We had a pod virtually to ourselves, just one other couple, and the whole of London at our feet.

What an exciting and memorable couple of days, and London buzzing with the Christmas spirit. But oh it was exhausting! Jon's energy levels were so low. Tired out now, we asked the taxi to take us earlier than we had planned. Jon collapsed into his train seat and slept on and off for the entire journey.

With all the excitement of the holiday and the trip to London, Jon was happy to have a low key celebration for his 26th birthday. A meal out together at the Bell was a sufficient treat.

Christmas 2011

Jon was keen to be well prepared for Christmas. He knew that illness could suddenly scupper well-laid plans and with that in mind he had a two-day break, by himself, in Bath in early November. He bought many of his Christmas presents, giving enormous thought to his choices. They were all very special gifts.

"I'd really like to my hut to be Christmassy this year," he announced, remembering last year when his Christmas hut plans had been abandoned. We joked about it being a Santa's grotto, complete with attractive young ladies dressed as little elves! That didn't happen, but after several trips to the garden centre his hut took on a very Christmassy look. He had holly berry lights and an illuminated snowman, fragrant candles, festoons of Christmas cards, and pride of place, the new nativity set. It looked wonderful and created a festive and joyful atmosphere. Jon was very happy with the results, especially when he and Roy went off to complete the picture with a real Christmas tree in a pot to stand just outside the door of the hut, ablaze with bright blue lights.

Jon was able to entertain many friends here over the Christmas period, especially Tom and Dawn. He felt well enough to go to church and on outings with friends and to the quiz nights at the Brimsham. It was a happy time.

Jon continued to eat well and thoroughly enjoyed his Christmas dinner. Rachel and Neill had come for Christmas, and had brought little table sparklers. It was a magical time at the dinner table, with the sparkling lights and candles shining on our happy family Christmas.

Jon also managed an outing on New Year's Eve. Stephen and Jon had celebrated New Year together on many occasions, this year they wandered across to the local pub, the Brimsham. I didn't expect that Jon would last until midnight, but I believe he managed to stay awake. 2012 was, after all, going to be a rather significant year. Did he know that at the time? I rather expect he did.

Chapter Nineteen

JON GOES ON
THE ROAD

2012

Before 2011 was out, Jon was already planning his adventures. His plans started to take shape as he researched places to go, transport and accommodation. His original idea was to travel down to the south coast, to make his way across to Rachel and Neill's in Bishops Stortford and from there to the most easterly point of the UK. He considered getting a flight from Stansted to Aberdeen, and then on to John O'Groats, or maybe Cape Wrath, the northernmost point of the UK. He had even got Dr Hopkins' permission to fly. I was not very popular, as to me the whole idea seemed over-ambitious. I suggested that he should leave travelling to northern Scotland until the summer. "I can't wait till summer, I have to go now!" he insisted. I didn't argue.

But then the idea started to fall apart. Jon discovered that he would have to cross London to get from Brighton to Bishops Stortford, and the idea appalled him. He decided that he would settle for an initial trip to Brighton to stay with Uncle Andy and Steph, and then travel along the south coast from there. I felt happier with this arrangement. He was at least starting somewhere familiar, with good company.

"But when are you coming back?" I wanted to know. He couldn't tell me. "Well, promise me, that just as soon as you feel that you'd rather be at home, you'll get straight on a train!" I insisted. He promised.

The day of departure came. Roy and I saw him onto the platform at Yate Station, loaded up with the heaviest backpack imaginable. Mostly it was his CPAP breathing machinery. Jon was delighted to discover that he could travel to Brighton on one train, with no changes – quite a surprise. Uncle Andy had agreed to meet him at the station when he arrived. So off he went, excited and nervous in equal measure, looking forward to his independence.

There were some slight problems on the journey when he was requested to put his backpack on the luggage rack. He couldn't lift it that high, so the train official did it for him. "But I won't be able to lift it down when I arrive" Jon reasoned. The man reassured him of some help. Of course he was nowhere to be seen when the time came and a panicky Jon thought the train would depart without him before he could struggle to retrieve the bag. Of course it didn't, but I can understand his anxiety.

The weekend with the family went very well. They enjoyed one another's company and Jon appreciated the attention, and the excursions. He was very well looked after. So far, so good.

Plans then emerged for his continuing journey. Hastings was chosen as his next stop. The *Rough Guide to the UK* listed the historical connections and Jon thought that all sounded very interesting. He chose a modest seafront hotel and found the train times. He rang me from Brighton station. "It has been lovely staying with Andy and Steph, but now I'm really excited to be stepping out on my own," he said.

Hastings in January is rather a forlorn kind of resort, grey, cold, and windswept, with lots of places (including his hotel) undergoing winter refurbishment. He soon tired of being there and made plans to travel to Chichester. This seemed to have an all-year-round appeal and sounded attractive. He loved it, and later urged Roy and me to visit it too.

He stayed at a pub called the Vestry, which had character and liveliness, and he thoroughly enjoyed being there. He also had the added bonus of an evening of easy company, and a welcome home-cooked meal with Neill's parents, Mary and David, who live in the town. The following day David entertained him with a guided tour, taking in the beautiful cathedral and the harbour.

Jon was considering his next move. He thought he might go on to Salisbury for the weekend, and asked me to look on the internet for him to research places to stay, and the train times. Then suddenly he had enough.

"Do you think I'd be a failure if I came home?" he asked me on the phone.

"Definitely not, you've done really well and should be very proud of yourself," I reassured him.

"Maybe I'll go to Salisbury another day," he sighed.

He came home the next day, totally exhausted but pleased with himself. It had been a challenge and he was proud of his achievement. I was overjoyed to see him. For me it had been a very, very long week. I was so relieved that he was home safe.

Jon developed a wide group of friends during his time at home, and considering his limited energy levels, he had a relatively active social life. During February he spent time with many of his friends. He loved his outings with Dawn. Her little red Mini took them to the seaside, where they walked along the winter beach, well wrapped up, laughing at each other's jokes and enjoying a wonderful friendship. On Tom's days off, he and Jon spent time together, sometimes bowling, sometimes going into Bristol. Despite the lateness he regularly went along to participate in the Sunday evening quiz nights at the Brimsham. He was a valuable addition to the quiz team with his football and music knowledge, but I think the attraction was largely due to Rebecca, with whom he teased and flirted. He had developed good friendships with the other members of the Hammer Out support group, and he enjoyed meeting up with them regularly.

Jon had always shown great support for my Mothers' Union work and often arrived at the meetings in church as it got to the tea and biscuits point. He was made very welcome by many of the ladies, and he enjoyed their (often grandmotherly) attention. Jon had joined previous outings to Dyrham Park and to Tewkesbury, but in February his interest moved up a gear. He took notice of the aims of the MU and felt some affinity with these. 'Christian Care for Families Worldwide' and the aim about supporting families in times of adversity struck a chord, and seemed important to him.

February is always a busy month for Mothers' Union and Jon got completely involved. He joined the group for lunch out at the Rose and Crown and also participated in the 'Wave of Prayer.'

"I think I'd like to be a member of the Mothers' Union, could I be?" he asked me,

"You know you could, Jon," I replied. We already had one male member and the Chief Executive, Reg Bailey, had been very much in the news.

Jon thought he would like to be more committed, and he offered to take on the job of organising the community minibus for outings. The next enrolment was scheduled for May. He put his name down.

February 2012 – MRI scan

Jon's appointment for his planned MRI scan came through on January 30th at 8.15am. We set off early to get through the morning rush hour to Frenchay. We checked in as usual and Jon filled in the obligatory health forms. For some reason he ticked the box marked 'kidney problems'. He had had to stop his original chemotherapy in 2003 due to his plummeting kidney function, but since then he had had nothing to worry about. I don't know if he usually ticked that box, but the radiographer decided on this occasion that he couldn't proceed with the scan until Jon had had a kidney function test.

Jon was so cross, he was fuming. He rarely expressed anger, but he was really frustrated by this. We both knew that the MRI scan would have to be completely re-scheduled, as would his follow up appointment with Dr Hopkins. It was not a good omen.

After a blood test showed that his kidneys were fine, the MRI scan finally took place on 9th February, with a new follow-up date of February 22nd at Frenchay Outpatients.

Rather as Jon had anticipated, it was not good news, and once again Dr Hopkins employed her small quiet voice.

"I'm afraid the tumour is regrowing" she said, "The neck is clear, but it is back in place in your brain." She showed us the image on the computer screen. Silence followed. There are no words.

Dr Hopkins offered further chemo, but also the opportunity to decline further treatment.

"I am not ready to throw in the towel just yet!" said Jon firmly and decisively. "When can I start the chemo?"

An appointment was made to attend the Oncology Centre on March 9th, to be checked over, and to collect the first round of Temozolomide chemotherapy tablets and some anti-sickness medication. It was a high dose. He knew he would feel rough, but it was a five-day course, then three weeks off. He felt sure he could handle it. 'I can do this!' He wrote in his diary. Three months of treatment were planned, then another scan. He was to start the course the following Tuesday, March 13th, my 60th birthday.

On Saturday 10th March Jon and I had a run out to The Mall at Cribbs Causeway. He wanted one or two things. I began to notice just how unsteady he had become. He was almost staggering, as if a little drunk. I caught his arm a couple of times, as it seemed he might fall.

"Perhaps you should start your chemo straight away?" I suggested. When we worked out the following dates and that the second course would start on Easter Sunday, we decided to leave things as they were.

"Perhaps I'm just a bit tired" Jon said to explain away his wobbliness.

I have to admit to being underwhelmed at the idea of my 60th birthday. I had no expectations, given that Jon was starting his chemo, I did not anticipate a celebratory jolliness to prevail. Well I was wrong, and very pleasantly surprised. What a wonderful day!

Jon had taken his tablets, then, complete with parcel, card and balloons, he had come cheerfully into our bedroom first thing in the morning. Jon had gone to enormous trouble, going into Bristol twice, to order and collect three tickets for the forthcoming Bristol Folk Festival. This was to be a three-day weekend event of folk singers and bands at the Colston Hall. It was to be held on the early May Bank Holiday. He was so excited to be giving them to me, as it was a complete surprise. He had also backed up the present by including a collection of CDs of music by some of the festival performers.

I had planned a small tea party for a few friends; we timed it so that Jon would be back from his singing lesson in time for the birthday cake. He was in great spirits and we were all able to enjoy my little party. We hadn't planned anything else, not knowing how Jon would be feeling, but he felt so good that we decided to go to the Swan at Nibley for a birthday meal. It was a wonderful, happy occasion, a lovely birthday after all.

Chapter Twenty

"THE CHEMO ISN'T WORKING"

March 2012

Jon finished the week of chemotherapy, feeling progressively worse as the week went on. "Never mind, I shall soon start feeling better" he stated, in his normal positive fashion.

A week later, we were preparing to go away. Jon was booked in to Tracy-Ann House in Bournemouth with his YCT friends. He was not up to the train journey, so we arranged to take him there and stay nearby in our caravan.

It was very uncertain whether we would go. Jon did not feel better, as he had anticipated, in fact, I know now that he felt pretty terrible. He was very wobbly and unsteady, and also quite emotional. He wasn't really sure whether he wanted to go, and he was upset and saddened. He admitted to me that he thought this might be the last time he would go.

In the morning, he decided that he would give it a try. He knew we were close by and that we could take him home at any point if he felt that he'd had enough. We set off, and now he had made a positive decision, the nervousness had gone and he was in good spirits. The journey was good, and having deposited our caravan we went on to deliver Jon to his destination.

He was so delighted to show us round. Roy and I had never been to Tracy-Ann House, and had only seen it in photographs. We were very impressed with the spaciousness and comfort, and its proximity to a beautiful sandy beach. We made a point of exchanging mobile phone numbers with several people at the house – just in case.

He managed very well; he even had a paddle in the sea! It was the most glorious warm and sunny week. For sure this was a gift from God at this very difficult time. Jon enjoyed the company of his friends and was able to participate in much more than he anticipated.

On Thursday we collected an exhausted Jon. He slept for the entire journey home. He was very glad that he had gone to Bournemouth, but he was oh so pleased to be home again.

Easter 2012

After a quiet Easter day, with a visit to church and not too much chocolate, Jon and I are looking forward to visiting our friends Liz and Juliet on Easter Monday.

The day starts badly, as Jon falls in the bathroom. He insists he is fine and by mid-morning we set off for Bitton. Just past Pucklechurch and Jon says he feels a bit sick.

"Shall I stop?" I suggest.

"No, I'll just open the window, I'll be fine in a minute," he reassures me.

Without warning he's suddenly projectile-vomiting, in and out of the car window. I stop quickly and try to clean up as best I can. I ring Juliet's mobile to let them know we won't be coming, then turn the car around and make our way home as hastily as is safe.

A ghastly-looking Jon flops down onto his bed. He agrees to me ringing the Oncology Centre. "Come in," they say "We need to check you over."

Jon is due to start the second cycle of chemotherapy the next day. The hospital doctor is unsure whether he is well enough. He has stopped being sick, but he is having a problem speaking clearly and he is very unsteady. In an attempt to stay upright, Jon launches himself towards his destination in a rush. The hospital physio tries to slow him down by lengthening his walking pole to 'crook' length. They also prescribe steroids, and he stays in overnight.

The next day he is so happy to come home. He misses his own bed and his mum's cooking. The steroids seem to help a bit and Dr Hopkins gives the go-ahead by email, so he is ready to start chemo again. He struggles through the next five days of Temozolomide, feeling awful all the time. His appointment to see Dr Hopkins is a week away.

The attractive dark-haired young lady on reception is clearly surprised to see the normally confident Jon now staggering into the building. She rushes to fetch a wheelchair. We sit together quietly in the colourful waiting area until Jon's name is called. Dr Hopkins appears, and we see the shock on her face. Then she utters the killer words that we had all been dreading, and deep down knew were coming eventually.

"I'm so sorry Jon, the chemo isn't working," she whispers. "You are too unwell to have any more treatment." She says she will arrange another scan, and will put the wheels in motion to organise a care plan and make a referral to St. Peter's Hospice.

I urge her to think of alternative treatments. "Is there anything else we could do, or could have done, anything overseas that might make a difference?"

She is sympathetic and lovely, and reassures us that she has left no stone unturned that might have made a difference. We talk about the bone marrow treatment that had always hovered about in the background, but she explains how she really doesn't believe that Jon's body would have tolerated that at all. She says kind things about us all and hugs us, but it is the end of the line. We didn't know it then, but we will not see her again.

The next morning Jon presents me with a sheet of paper, torn from his notebook.

"What's this?" I ask.

"A list of meals I would like," replies the ever-practical Jon. I think he is being overly dramatic, but I take notice of his requests and plan the following week's menu accordingly. One request in particular stands out in my memory. He wanted to order take-away pizza. He wanted a feast, and I was not allowed to comment on his choices, or quantities! Dare I admit that Roy and I had never had take-away pizza before?

The pizza surpasses Jon's expectations and we have a wonderful evening. It's a real party. We all eat far too much, but Jon thoroughly enjoys every minute.

The community physiotherapist and occupational therapist come to see Jon again. They provide some extra, necessary help. We already have a banister rail and a bath board in place, and now they bring a walking frame on wheels, a sort of harness and a bed lever. We practise going up and down the stairs with the special harness, me following behind and hanging onto him.

They suggest a wheelchair. Jon fancies a racing model with go-faster stripes, but we settle for a loan one from the Red Cross for the time being. We test the wheelchair the next day at the St. George's Day lunch at St. Mary's Church. Pushing him in the wheelchair from the car park in the school playground, although only a slight incline, really challenges my muscles!

People are pleased to see us, but there are some shocked faces when they see Jon in the wheelchair, and particularly when he attempts to transfer to a normal seat. He is pleased to be back in church, he hadn't been well enough to go to the Sunday services for some while, and he feels comfortable and relaxed amongst friends in that special place.

Getting to Jon's hut has become a struggle too. I am concerned that if he falls on the way there or back, he may go through the conservatory windows. However, it remains a haven and it is worth the effort of getting there. He watches films with Dawn, entertains both Juliet and Tom, relaxes and sleeps.

It is also the perfect place to be close to God, and we have our own little acts of worship, just Jon and I. We have been given a number of very relevant prayer books, so with those, the Bible, and a CD of favourite 'Songs of Praise', we light a candle and worship quietly together.

Monday 23rd April 2012

"I want to go to Bath," declares Jon, once he is up and dressed.

"It's raining cats and dogs!" I protest.

"I still want to go to Bath."

"Wouldn't it be better to go another day?" I suggest hopefully,

"No, I want to go today!"

We go to Bath.

It is very hard work pushing the now heavy Jon around the uneven pavements of Bath. Bath was most definitely not designed for wheelchairs. There is a great lack of crossing points, and nearly all the shops have entrance steps of some kind. It is also quite steep in places. The rain doesn't stop either, it just keeps steadily pouring down upon us.

Jon has a purpose for wanting to go into Bath. He has decided that he wants to buy his good friend Tom a T-shirt with a printed slogan for his birthday, and he knows of a shop in Bath that does this. He is also determined to go down the steep and uneven steps to the old sweet shop, to fill a jar with a selection of chocolate mints, also for Tom's birthday. His abandoned wheelchair, at the top of the steps, becomes completely soaked whilst he is in the shop. The sweet ladies rush out with kitchen roll to dry it for him.

They are less helpful in Patisserie Valerie, one of the few eating places without steps. It is still difficult to access and the disabled toilet is right at the back of the café. We are a real nuisance pushing past people's chairs and shopping bags to get to the toilet. It is a difficult day. But the mission is accomplished, even though I am embarrassed to admit that I am a grumpy companion, and for that I'm eternally sorry.

On the journey home from Bath, we have a conversation about our bathroom. Jon confides that getting in and out of the bath for a shower, even with the bath board in place, is becoming increasingly difficult. We have seen advertisements for a disabled shower that can be fitted 'in a day' in the space of an existing bath. Jon is keen to investigate this and I agree that it would certainly help.

Later that afternoon I ring the number. The very obliging person on the phone makes an appointment for the salesman to come the following day.

Tuesday 24th April 2012

Today is the day scheduled for the MRI scan at Frenchay. It is an effort to be ready and there in time, but we make it. The wheelchair doesn't fit into the crowded waiting room, so Jon is directed to the corridor. He is so tired; he is uncomfortable sitting and is desperate to lie down. Over an hour later, he is taken to the scanner. It is a real ordeal.

At lunchtime Joanne, now a licensed lay-minister, arrives. She brings the Eucharist to Jon at home. We sit in the lounge with calm music playing and light candles to set the scene. We feel blessed and strengthened by this Holy Communion, and sense the presence of God with us.

By afternoon Jon is too weary to climb the stairs. He decides to rest instead in his hut. There is a wobbly journey to get there, but then he falls into a deep sleep on his settee. He is still fast asleep when the Aquability salesman calls. We don't want to wake him, so Roy and I discuss our needs with the man. We are able to bring the suggested fitting date forward from four weeks to two, so we sign the agreement. We want to make sure that we are doing everything we can to make life easier. Jon is disappointed to have missed the discussion, but is happy with what we have chosen.

PART FIVE
THE END

Chapter Twenty One

ST. PETER'S HOSPICE

Friday 27th April 2012

Roy has arrived in advance of the ambulance and is waiting for us when we arrive. The ambulance draws up at the back doors and Jon is wheeled into the light and airy building. Two friendly and welcoming nurses come to meet us.

Jon is awake now, but drowsy. He settles happily into a bed with lovely fresh blue sheets. He can just make out the garden through the windows by his side. It is a big room with another bed, as yet unfilled across on the far side. It is bright and clean.

Someone brings us all a cup of tea. Jon seems relaxed and almost content.

The doctor comes to talk to us all. She tells us that she has the results of Jon's scan if we would like to talk about them. Jon doesn't want to; we decide to leave that discussion until the morning.

Jon tucks into a beautifully presented dinner and enjoys it. We all recognise that Jon has arrived at a safe place. It is beautiful and welcoming. The nurses are very friendly and kind.

With phones charged and contact details established, we kiss our darling boy bye-bye, and make our heavy-hearted way home.

Week One

We are met as we arrive in the morning by the Sister on duty. She tells us that Jon attempted to go to the nearby toilet on his own in the night and fell heavily, bumping his forehead. This had caused some concern, so they have decided he needs to have somebody with him at all times. When we leave him, a nurse will come and sit with him until we return. It is a great comfort to us that he isn't alone at any time.

A different doctor is on duty in the morning. He is clearly nervous of telling us the awful truth, and skirts round the subject of Jon's scan result. We are not surprised that the tumour has grown quite a bit. We can see the results of it for ourselves, glaringly obvious. The doctor doesn't know how much to tell Jon, but Jon does.

"Stop!" he says to the doctor, "don't tell me any more!" He agrees that the doctor can talk to his mum and dad.

The doctor continues to talk to us outside Jon's room, but he isn't really saying anything, he is just making us feel very uncertain and nervous of what will happen next.

A room-mate arrives. He is a pleasant man, but obviously in a lot of pain as he groans a lot. Every time he groans, Jon grumbles under his breath "Oh shut up!" Jon is not impressed with groaning.

He is, however, exceedingly impressed with the food. He can't wait to tell me as I arrive on the first morning that he has had a full English cooked breakfast. Jon can also choose what he would like for his lunch and dinner. There are three courses with a choice in each course! It is all attractively presented on a tray with a doily and a small posy of flowers. The food is all cooked freshly and Jon really appreciates this. He loves having puddings too, especially traditional favourites like sponge pudding and custard. A real treat!

Actually getting the food from the plate to his mouth presents a problem though. Rachel suggests 'contour cutlery' specially designed and shaped to help. She brings some with her for Jon to try and the Hospice also search for special cutlery to make eating easier. I'm not sure if any of it helps. Eventually Jon has to accept help from me with eating. It becomes evident that he can't see what is on his plate, so as I help him, I also announce the food that is on its way, and ask him to choose what he would like for his next mouthful.

Jon doesn't much like being helped. Early on in his stay a nurse remarked "He's fiercely independent, isn't he!" Perhaps she was unused to helping a 26-year-old in the bathroom. Of course he is independent; he does not want to be helped at all! Help is better coming from professionals though, particularly when it comes to personal care. He would have hated to have been helped to shower by his parents. He gradually accepts nursing help. The bathroom is just across the corridor from his room and it is designed to be able to accommodate wheelchairs with easy access to the toilet and a spacious wet room. Jon appreciates these facilities; he is always happiest when he is clean and tidy.

During this first week Jon is quite laid back, and very sleepy. He seems to be in a happy world of his own most of the time. He astounds us with some amazingly profound statements and unusual vocabulary. He likes to amuse us and he chuckles at his own jokes. Without the growth-reducing effects of chemotherapy, his hair and beard begin to grow. He remarks that he is very proud of his beard. He doesn't want it trimmed, thank you very much! It starts to look a little wild, and he likes it.

Lots of visitors come on that first Sunday. The now pregnant Rachel and Neill arrive at home on the Saturday evening so in the morning we all go to the Hospice for visiting time at 11am. Jon is very pleased to see us and teases Rachel about her bump, calling the baby 'turnip' (apparently the baby is about the size of a turnip around this time) or sometimes 'heavenly turnip peace lily'! Egged on by Neill, he also jokes about Rachel having a 'hairy tummy', which of course she doesn't have at all, but we all laugh anyway!

Soon Andy and Steph arrive too, all the way from Hove. Jon thoroughly enjoys the attention and visiting time takes on a party atmosphere. Andy and Steph reminisce about his visit to them in January, and tell some funny stories. Steph remarks that Jon seems very much 'at peace'.

By the afternoon Jon doesn't feel so good. The visitors have gone now and he is exhausted from the effort of entertaining them, much as he did enjoy it. He drifts in and out of sleep.

After the weekend we are pleased that Doctor Ruth is back in charge. She has such a lovely warm and friendly manner and Jon likes her. We meet Zena the Consultant as well, who comes on Mondays and Thursdays. She talks a lot of sense and I am impressed by her. We have a long discussion on the first Thursday. I ask her about Emily. "Jon has a sister in New Zealand; she wants to be here but has limited time off, what should I be telling her?" I ask. Her thoughtful answer suggests that it might be time to start making a move, as it will obviously take several days to get here. I relay the message to Emily that evening, saying, "Don't panic, but it might be time to think about getting a flight". Emily texts me in the morning "flight booked, see you next Wednesday".

All week I am careful not to mention the word 'folk' in case Jon remembers that he has bought tickets for the Folk Festival and questions me about it. I know that he will be upset about missing it. Out of the blue on Saturday morning he asks me "What day is it?" Reluctantly I admit to it being Saturday. "When is the Folk Festival?" he asks urgently. I hesitate and he insists on an answer. I have to tell him that it is this weekend.

"Aren't you going to it then?" he asks plaintively,

"No Jon, I want to be here, I don't want to be anywhere else!"

He is upset, just as I feared.

Later that afternoon he is upset again. Suddenly he seems to be more aware of his situation. It is as though a mist has cleared. Gemma, a friend from Worcester who he had got to know at the YCT holidays in Bournemouth, has been to see him. He is very pleased to see her and welcomes her warmly. They chat happily and look at some photos together that she has brought from the YCT holiday the previous September. I think they may have made him think about all the things he wouldn't be doing any more. After Gemma has gone we share some tears. It is unusual for Jon to cry, but also totally reasonable. My heart is tearing into shreds.

It doesn't put him off having visitors though; he loves it when people come. During the first week he has lots of visits, from Dawn, from Tom, from his singing teacher Jane, from Bryony who had struggled on the bus from Bristol to get there, from Kate, from Julie and a prayerful visit from Joanne and Louisa. He loves them all. Every day he asks, "Who is coming to see me today?" He makes a great effort to be pleasant and even funny, even though it is hard for him to talk and he is so tired.

Week Two

The second weekend is the Bank Holiday. Up until now I have been abiding by the suggested visiting times and arriving at about 11 o'clock each morning. On Thursday Sister Jan asks me if I can come in earlier as she has a staffing problem. Could I come at 8.30 or 9 am? I am delighted! I soon realise what I have been missing. Jon is awake early and is up, showered, dressed and having his breakfast as I arrive. Coming early I see him at his brightest, enjoying his bacon and egg. He is so pleased to see me. I realise what a long time it has been for him to wait until 11, as by then he is tired and ready to go back to bed. There is no going back for me. I come in as early as possible every day from then on.

Coming early gives more opportunities for outings too.

The grounds are beautiful and designed for accessibility. He calls them 'My Grounds' and he loves to go outside, especially when we can sit for a while in the sun in a sheltered part of the garden. We chat easily and he tells me how lovely it is here. He is relaxed and knows that he is in a good place; he compares it very favourably with all the hospitals where he has been a patient, and counts himself lucky. He loves to feel the fresh air on his skin and he delights in the smell of the wallflowers, lavender and herbs.

From inside we can see a variety of pretty songbirds and a squirrel, feeding from the nuts and seeds at the bird table. We are thrilled to see a nuthatch. Jon cannot see them, but we tell him about them and he is pleased.

Jon increasingly cannot see things, but he insists on wearing his watch, and having his phone and PSP portable gaming station close by even though I am convinced that he can't see them. He has no interest in television. He loves his music though. The paramedic who brought him into the Hospice suggested that he brought some CDs. He brought Newton Faulkner's *Hand Built by Robots*, Beth Rowley's *Little Dreamer* and Christie Moore's *Folk Tale*. In the first week he played Newton Faulkner over and over again. One day he asks me to put on *The Lord is my Shepherd* from the *Songs of Praise* CD, so now that joins the others along with Emily Smith's *Traiveller's Joy*. I love to watch him listening to Christie Moore's *My Little Honda*

50. It has a catchy tune and Jon taps his feet rhythmically and with enthusiasm. I cry quietly to myself though as we listen to Emily Smith as she sings plaintively 'I will take you home', as I know I can't do that. I can read to him though and he loves that, especially poetry, so now we have a good collection of poetry books lined up on the window sill. Some are funny and some thoughtful, a good mixture.

We have some good outings inside the building too. He loves to visit the music room, with its array of percussion instruments; he tentatively strikes the bongo drums and the xylophone and grins cheekily. Then we move on to the Sanctuary, a beautiful peaceful room with a stained-glass window with a picture of a weeping tree beside a babbling stream. We light a candle on the votive stand under the window, and then we sit together in silence, drinking in the tranquillity of the scene. There are Bibles nearby and Jon asks me to read to him; he especially loves Psalm 23. He leans back in his wheelchair and closes his eyes whilst I read: 'The Lord is my Shepherd, I shall not want, He makes me lie down in green pastures; He leads me besides still waters; he restores my soul. He leads in me in paths of righteousness for His name's sake. Even though I walk through the valley of the shadow of death, I fear no evil; for Thou art with me; Thy rod and thy staff they comfort me.'

When asked on admission to the hospice, Jon had said

that he was a Christian, and that a visit from the Chaplain would be welcomed. Early in the second week, Chaplain Bert comes to see him. He comes when I am not there, and Jon tells me about him. It seems they got on well. Bert is surprised and impressed by Jon's calm acceptance of his situation and his strong faith. He comes again later especially to see me. He tells me of the conversation he has had with Jon and how Jon's main concern is for his Mum and Dad. Jon is worried about us. Bert comes again several times. He is shocked and upset by Jon's young age. He prays with us and it comforts us.

On the second Sunday, before Bert's visiting begins, we have our own simple service at Jon's bedside. I play *The Lord is my Shepherd* from the *Songs of Praise* CD, Jon holds his wooden holding cross, I read some prayers and readings from the little books that Rev. Judith Lee has sent us and say some personal prayers, asking God for strength and peace for Jon and for us, and saying thank you for the blessings we are receiving by being there, for the beauty of the place and the exceptional care. Roy is aware that Jon's room-mate Tony is showing great interest and is hanging on to every word. We hope he may have got some strength from it too.

The next day the opportunity comes to move into a single room. This room has the benefit of its own toilet too and Jon is very happy about that.

At this point Jon is only having steroids and his normal medication. His headaches start to become more persistent. Doctor Ruth suggests that a regular dose of paracetamol would be helpful. Until now Jon has had it only by request. He agrees that this may help.

By Wednesday the regular paracetamol doesn't seem to be quite enough either, so the stronger co-codamol is added to his prescription. He is so tired but he is also restless and fidgety, a sure sign of pain breaking through.

Another room becomes available. This room is bigger and has an en-suite with a walk-in shower. It has a beautiful outlook and doors into the garden. Doctor Ruth sits beside Jon as she tells him about the other room and suggests that he may prefer it.

"I just wish I could go home and go in my own bed," Jon sighs.

"Do you think you would feel better in your own bed?" Doctor Ruth asks sensitively,

"No," admits Jon, "I think I am better here!"

He is aware that he needs the care that is available to him at the Hospice, but he is sad. Doctor Ruth suggests that we make Jon's new room as Jon-like as we can. It seems like a good plan and we set about creating a home from home with pictures and cards stuck on the wardrobe doors, big and little Tiggers on his bed and the red crochet throw from his hut draped on his chair. Rainbow tulips now stand on the window sill with his books of poetry. It looks cosy, colourful and personal.

Before I go home on Wednesday I tell Jon that he should be having a special visitor tomorrow. "Who?" he asks, "Is it Billy and Kate?"

"No!" I retort, "Not royalty. But this person is coming on an aeroplane, a long way, especially to see you."

"Ooh!" he grins, "It's Emmy!"

He is pleased that his speech, which had been such a problem, seems to be improving. Communication with everyone is, surprisingly, becoming easier. He was so frustrated when we couldn't understand him. His sight, however, is worse; he says, "I wish I could see more!" I hug him sympathetically. It is all I can do.

Chapter Twenty Two

EMILY COMES HOME

Emily arrives amid chaos! Rachel and Neill have agreed to meet her from Heathrow airport and bring her home. They are earlier than we expect and we don't have enough dinner to go round. The bathroom has been started that day, and despite their claims to replace the bath and install a shower 'in a day', of course that is not the case and bathroom debris lies in and around the house. What a dreadful welcome for a weary traveller from the other side of the world. I am finding the whole situation too much to handle and away from the hospice I can't stop crying.

After a night's sleep we are ready to face the next day. Jon is so delighted to see Emily. He jokes and teases her, just like old times. He is so proud to show her round 'his place'! Rachel and Neill come to visit too on Thursday morning and Jon loves the fuss and attention and there is a happy atmosphere. He calls us all different varieties of sausage, and says that we are 'splendiferous'!

For two days Emily stays close by. She reads to him and draws pictures to stick on the wall. They joke and laugh, and Emily sits quietly in his chair as he sleeps.

Saturday 12th May

On Saturday morning I go in alone. Emily decides she needs to go to the bank and buy some essential bits and pieces. She will come in later with Roy.

I read some poetry to Jon and then we listen to some music for a while.

"Can we go out?" Jon asks. It is a fine morning, so we get the wheelchair and I wrap Jon up warmly. As we are about to go through the door the Reverend Iain Macfarlane arrives. He joins us in the grounds. Jon is pleased to see Rev. Iain and is keen to show him around. We sit in the sunshine and they chat companionably. Jon wants to show Iain 'The Sanctuary' so we head indoors to the beautiful room with the stained glass window. We light a candle and sit quietly. Jon and Iain talk about the Bible, and Jon tells him how his favourite reading is Psalm 23. Rev. Iain reads the psalm from one of the Bibles in the room, and then another favourite, Psalm 46. 'God is our refuge, our help in the trials that would crush us.' He prays with us.

"That was wonderful!" Jon says in a dreamy voice as we leave this spiritual place.

We make our way back to Jon's room to find that it is lunchtime, so we bid farewell to Iain and Jon thanks him warmly for coming. His visit has really made a difference. Jon enjoys his lunch, but is then very tired and is helped into bed and sleeps.

Later Emily and Roy arrive. Emily has bought some cooked cocktail sausages, and the old sausage jokes re-emerge. But Jon is not very comfortable and is too tired to even sit up for some tea. He does manage a couple of the sausages though.

Sunday 13th May

As soon as I see Jon on Sunday morning, I can tell straight away that he doesn't feel well. He is wearing his glasses and a serious expression and he is sitting in his chair. I can see that he is pleased to see me, but there is a clear difference in his demeanour. He says he would like to go outside in the wheelchair again, but he is rather tired, so he thinks he'll have a bit of a sleep first. He is helped to get back into bed. He tosses and turns in bed and can't get comfortable.

His medication now includes an oral morphine drug. It is decided to increase the dose and now he sleeps deeply, right through his Sunday lunch. He is fitful when he wakes, his legs shake and he shouts out. Emily and I are frightened by his reactions and call the nurses each time. They call them 'episodes' and give him calming medication. He is awake enough for a little supper of mashed potato and some yogurt, but he coughs and chokes on it.

Week 3
Monday 14th May

In the morning Roy and I have an appointment with Doctor Zena and Doctor Ruth together. They explain that it would seem to be the time for Jon to be fitted with a syringe driver so that medication for pain relief, morphine, sedatives and steroids can all be administered regularly. We agree readily; we just want Jon to be as comfortable as possible.

"Are you staying here?" asks Doctor Ruth,

"No," I reply, "Should I be doing?"

They ascertain that the family room is available and we are invited to move into it today. Doctor Zena also suggests, in the kindest way possible, that Jon may have only a few days left, or it could even be just a few hours.

Roy goes home to collect some overnight belongings, and to keep up with Jon's washing that he has lovingly been doing each day. Jon has had a constant supply of the quirky, colourfully-patterned fun pyjamas that are his day and night attire of choice.

I ring Rachel at work in Bishops Stortford and she leaves at once, to make her way straight to the Hospice. Jon relaxes into a deep, drug-induced sleep.

As darkness falls, Rachel and Emily at last depart the Hospice for home together, leaving Roy and me behind for the night.

Chapter Twenty Three

THE LONGEST WEEK

Dawn comes to see Jon. She is going on holiday to Venice tomorrow and she wants to come in before she goes. She has been such a caring and consistent friend, visiting Jon regularly throughout. Jon sleeps through her visit, but she talks to him and says goodbye. She and I sit in the café and shed many tears together before she leaves.

On Tuesday morning Jon wakes very briefly. He recognises my voice and cries out, "Mum!" He lifts his arms towards me for a hug and we embrace. It is very emotional and I try to contain my distress.

At intervals over the next few days, Jon requires greater amounts of pain relief. He has short fidgety moments, but mostly he sleeps peacefully. I pad up and down the corridor in my slippers during the night to watch Jon sleeping. He doesn't move.

Every morning the girls arrive. We are together in Jon's room. Sometimes the emotional and pregnant Rachel goes to the family room for a sleep, as the situation overwhelms her. We take turns to go for walks through the fields around the Hospice. The fresh air and the opportunity to stretch my legs restores me. We drink tea and eat in the café, without tasting the cakes and sandwiches. Time passes slowly without interruption as we pretend to read magazines and books.

On Thursday evening there is a change. Jon is coughing and he breathes noisily. There is a cry in his every breath. It is a heart-breaking sound. A nurse tops up his calming medicine and the crying sound subsides. I decide to sit beside him through the night. I feel sure that the end must be near. I sit in a chair watching his chest heave up and down. Roy is dozing in the recliner, but at two o'clock he gives in and makes his way back to the bedroom to get some sleep. There is a spare hospital bed in the corner of the room, so I lie on it, but I continue to watch my sleeping boy. Every now and then Jon coughs and I jump up.

Friday 18th May

Eventually morning comes and there is no real change. Roy and I are ushered out of Jon's room so that the nurses can give him a wash to freshen him up. When we return

Jon has visibly deteriorated. His face is ashen and his breathing rasps. I am shocked and distressed by his appearance. I text the girls: 'Don't come in today!' Rachel was very upset yesterday, and I worry about her seeing Jon like this. They, of course, ignore me.

As I sit beside Jon, I cry a silent but angry prayer to God. "Where are you? Jon is suffering, what are you doing?" I implore.

Roy sits in the recliner chair across the room. The clock ticks in the silence. Then, without warning, in the peaceful calm and quiet of the room, Jon's breathing just stops.

"He's stopped breathing," I whisper needlessly. Roy is already by my side; Jon breathes again, then stops. Then again. I look at the clock; it is a quarter to ten.

As we wait, hushed, for another breath, Chaplain Bert walks into the room and immediately behind him are our girls. We all gather round Jon's bed, and encircle with love the peaceful, beautiful, still body of our darling boy.

Bert prays fervently. God's presence surrounds us.

There is absolutely no doubt that our beloved Jon is now in God's loving hands.

At peace.

Battle over.

POSTSCRIPT

Jon's cremated remains are buried in St Mary's Churchyard in Yate. Living reminders of Jon's life are to be found in two places that were special to Jon. At Westonbirt Arboretum we have adopted a mature Acer palmatum tree in Jon's name, and at the National Trust's Dyrham Park we planted a young horse chestnut tree in his memory.

In May 2013 Roy and I set up a supporter group with the Brain Tumour Charity in Jon's name: 'The Brain Tumour Charity – Jon Fredrickson Fund'.

Brain tumours are the biggest cancer killer of children and adults under 40, yet research is woefully under-funded. The Brain Tumour Charity is the largest dedicated funder of research into brain tumours in the UK, committed to finding new treatments and better diagnosis techniques.

We are hopeful that this investment in research will improve the outcomes and quality of life of all those diagnosed with a brain tumour in the future.

By purchasing this book you will have helped to make a difference. To donate please visit:

www.thebraintumourcharity.org/
supporter-groups/Jon-Fredrickson-Fund